BEAUTIFUL BEACHCOMBERS
SHOREBIRDS

ACKNOWLEDGMENTS

Thanks to Kevin Karlson for critiquing Chapters 5 and 6, to Brian Harrington for commenting on Chapter 10, to Debbie Pankonin for proofreading various drafts on this manuscript, and especially to Paul Lehman for carefully reviewing the entire work. The responsibility for any errors, however, lies with the author. Thanks also to Tom Vezo, Kevin Karlson (again), and the other photographers who generously contributed their splendid shorebird photographs to this project.

To learn more about Arthur Morris visit: *www.birdsasart.com*

Additional photography © 1996:
Tom Vezo, 12, 44-45, 60, 90-91, 98-99, 127, 154-55; Michael P. Gage, 13, 130-31; Kevin T. Karlson, 40, 52, 53, 54, 58-59, 104-5, 123; Charles Krebs, 76-77; Brian E. Small, 89; John Gerlach/Visuals Unlimited, 100; Richard Crossley, 108; Doug Wechsler/Vireo, 129; Hannu Hautala, 133; Johann Schumacher, 138.

Additional photo captions:
Half Title page: American Avocet in breeding plumage; Dedication page: Black-bellied Plover in nonbreeding plumage; Table of Contents page: Pacific Golden-Plover molting to nonbreeding plumage; Pages 154 and 155: American Oystercatchers; Page 157: Red Knots and Ruddy Turnstones in breeding plumage.

Illustrations on pages 18 and 19 © 1996, Julie Zickefoose

Book design by Kenneth Hey

Published by
STACKPOLE BOOKS
5067 Ritter Road
Mechanicsburg, PA 17055
www.stackpolebooks.com

Printed in China

10 9 8 7 6 5 4 3 2 1

Third edition

Originally published by NorthWood Press in 1996.

Library of Congress Cataloging-in-Publication Data

Morris, Arthur, 1946–
    Shorebirds : beautiful beachcombers / Arthur Morris.—3rd ed.
      p. cm.
    "Originally published : Minocqua : NorthWood Press, Inc., 1996."
    Includes bibliographical references (p.).
    ISBN 0-8117-2619-3
     1. Shorebirds—North America. I. Title.

QL696C4 M67 2003
598.3'3'097—dc21

2002026651

BEAUTIFUL BEACHCOMBERS
SHOREBIRDS

by Arthur Morris

STACKPOLE
BOOKS

This book is dedicated to the memory of my loving, supportive wife, Elaine Belsky-Morris. Elaine, who thought she would never be able to identify a Black-bellied Plover in winter plumage (but did), passed away on November 20, 1994.

TABLE OF CONTENTS

INTRODUCTION 9

Chapter 1   IDENTIFYING SHOREBIRDS 1 5

Chapter 2   PLUMAGES AND AGEING 2 5

Chapter 3   BEHAVIOR 3 3

Chapter 4   FEEDING AND DIET 4 3

Chapter 5   MATING AND BREEDING 4 9

Chapter 6   EGGS AND YOUNG 6 3

Chapter 7   MIGRATION 6 9

Chapter 8   SPECIES ACCOUNTS 7 6

Chapter 9   SHOREBIRDING 1 4 3

Chapter 10   CONSERVATION 1 4 7

              FOR MORE INFORMATION 1 5 6

              SUGGESTED READING 1 5 8

              PHOTO INDEX 1 6 0

Marbled Godwit in breeding plumage

INTRODUCTION

I t was a still, steamy mid-August morning. The southbound migrant bird stood on a mud flat at the Jamaica Bay Wildlife Refuge in Queens, New York. Its cinnamon-buff feathers shone brilliantly in golden sunlight.

Through borrowed binoculars, I saw that half of the bird's long, gently upcurved bill was black. But I couldn't help staring at the base of its bill—an exquisite shade of alabaster pink. "How could such a beautiful bird exist in New York City?" I wondered.

Unbeknown to me, my encounter with that single bird would dramatically change the course of the remainder of my adult life.

More than two decades later, this time on a prairie in central Montana,
I stared once again at the bill of what I now recognized as a Marbled Godwit,
and once again, stood transfixed. Through the barrel of my 800mm telephoto
lens, I saw that the tip of this godwit's bill was also black, but that the base was
a haunting shade of orange that I had never seen before.

I had, on three North American coasts, observed hundreds, even thousands
of Marbled Godwits since that first one had stolen my soul more than twenty
years ago. And each and every one of them had a *pink*-based bill.

But *this* Marbled Godwit had an *orange*-based bill. Why? The bird was in full
breeding plumage, when the color of a bird's soft parts (its bill, legs, and feet) is
often changed or enhanced by increased hormonal levels. Thus, an orange-
based bill for this godwit, and an added bit of shorebird knowledge for me.

For the most part, shorebirds are small and brown. And many species have
a great affection for mud—the blacker and the gooier, the better. Why then are so
many natural history enthusiasts the world over enthralled by the study of this
apparently—at first glance—oh-so-ordinary group?

First is their true beauty. Sandpipers, which make up the bulk of North
American shorebird species, are—in fresh breeding and in fresh juvenal
plumage—strikingly handsome, their earth-toned feathers, strikingly patterned.
The sandpiper palette includes black, white, and gray; orange, red-orange,
orange-red, and brick red; buff, tan, cream, and countless shades of brown.

Even more beautiful than the sandpipers are the larger North American
shorebirds. In breeding plumage the large plovers are spangled black, white,
and silver, and in several species, greenish or yellowish gold. Oystercatchers
feature large, bright red or orange bills. The Black-necked Stilt, with its amazingly
long pink legs, is rivaled in elegance only by the American Avocet with its long
blue legs, buff-orange hood, and sweepingly upcurved bill.

The second reason for the popularity of shorebirds is their diversity—diversity
in size, shape, and structure; diversity in diet and in feeding and migratory strate-
gies; and diversity in breeding behaviors.

Species diversity is great as well. As of this writing, 89 species of shorebirds
have occurred in North America. Of these, 48 breed regularly on the continent.
Nearly all the rest are vagrants, shorebirds from other continents that wander or
become lost while on migration.

A third reason for our fascination with shorebirds is the fantastic migrations
that many of these tiny bits of fluff and feather undertake each year. Several
species of North American shorebirds, weighing just a few ounces on average, winter
in South America, some routinely reaching as far south as the Straits of Magellan.
And while some may never wander far from the place where they hatched, others

Stilt Sandpiper in breeding plumage

fly more than 20,000 miles round-trip annually.

The fourth factor involved in the popularity of shorebirds (especially among birders) is the challenge of identifying them correctly. To the beginning shorebirder, those small brownish birds with white bellies scurrying madly about a mud flat all look the same.

Red-necked Stint in breeding plumage

I remember marveling at the skills of the late Thomas H. Davis, Jr., as he peered through his 10x40 binoculars at a group of small sandpipers more than a hundred yards distant. "Left to right," he would intone, "two adult White-rumps, a juvenile Semi, four Leasts—one a worn adult, and there, on the right, a juvenile Baird's. See the buffy face and the crossed wingtips?"

"He *must* be making it up," I thought at the time. Within half a decade, though, I found myself able to identify most shorebird species at forty yards—without binoculars.

Reason number five: Migrant shorebirds travel such great distances that navigational errors of only a few degrees can result in their reaching the "wrong" continent. Each year, vagrant shorebirds from Europe and Asia are found in North America by competent observers; and these occurrences cause great excitement in the birding community.

In late July 1985, the morning after being alerted to the presence of a strange sandpiper by friends, I located and identified New York State's first known Red-necked Stint on the East Pond at the Jamaica Bay Wildlife Refuge. This tiny shorebird breeds primarily in Siberia and winters chiefly in southeast Asia and Australasia. The stint stayed at the East Pond for nearly three weeks; birders from 17 states traveled to the Big Apple to view this vagrant shorebird and add it to their "life lists" of bird sightings.

North America's first known Little Curlew visited Santa Maria, California, in the fall of 1984. It apparently had taken a wrong turn while en route from its interior Siberian breeding grounds to its wintering grounds in northern Australia.

The tiny curlew settled in a pasture belonging to a Mr. & Mrs. Mahoney. The Mahoneys relocated their cows, opened the pasture gates, and played host to more than 400 birders from 18 states. The bird stayed almost a month, so nearly all the birders went home happy.

All who pursue shorebirds share a common bond: each of us has stood countless times on desolate beaches or flats and watched a flock of sandpipers flashing dark and light, twisting and turning in synchronous flight. And each time this happens, we are filled with a sense of awe and wonder.

Wilson's Phalarope female in breeding plumage

IDENTIFYING SHOREBIRDS

Chapter

1

horebird identification isn't nearly as difficult as most people think. By spending time in the field on a regular basis, studying a good field guide, and keeping company with an experienced shorebirder or two, it is fairly easy to come to know the common birds and their various plumages. As a result, picking out and putting names to the more unusual species becomes easier as well.

Jamaica Bay Wildlife Refuge, Queens, NY

F I E L D   G U I D E S

While there are several guides on the market for the beginning birder, no single guide does a good job of depicting the breeding, nonbreeding, and juvenal plumages of shorebirds. There are a few, however, with many species portrayed fairly accurately in all three plumages. Be sure to look at all the guides carefully before selecting one, or a combination of several, that allow you to identify birds in the various plumages.

Once you've purchased a field guide, spend lots of time thumbing through the shorebird section. Study the shapes of the various birds. Look closely at the bills (but not too closely—shorebird bills are almost always drawn *too thin* in field guides that use paintings). Note size comparisons. Read the text. Learn the key field marks. Study the differences between similar species. Study the range maps and note which birds are to be expected in your area.

T I M E   A F I E L D

There is no substitute for experience. The more time you spend in the field observing shorebirds, the more proficient you will become at identifying them.

Join a natural history or birding club in your area. These organizations conduct trips to nearby birding areas; some of the sites that they visit may attract large numbers of shorebirds at various times of the year. Attend as many of these trips as possible. The leaders are usually experienced birders. If you don't own a spotting scope, there are usually several to be shared by the group. Ask lots of questions about identification, ageing, the timing of migration, and about any shorebirds that breed locally.

At the conclusion of your first full season of serious shorebirding, you'll feel quite confident about identifying most of the regularly occurring species. When the next season rolls around, however, you'll feel lost and confused at first— you'll have difficulty sorting out even the common sandpipers. Try not to get too frustrated; within a week or two you'll find that your old skills have quickly returned. After several years, though, you'll find yourself able to quickly nail the

identification of most of the birds that you see, even on the first field outing of a new season.

By visiting regional shorebird sites regularly, you'll surely meet a master shorebirder or two. Most will be willing to share their knowledge with you. Not only will they be able to help you improve your identification skills, but they may direct you to additional shorebirding locales nearby.

ID BASICS

There are only four shorebird families regularly represented in North America. Birds in Recurvirostridae, the avocet and stilt family, have long, thin bills and long legs. In Haematopodidae, the oystercatcher family, each species has a large, laterally flattened bill. These two families are very distinctive and easily recognized.

SHOREBIRD TOPOGRAPHY

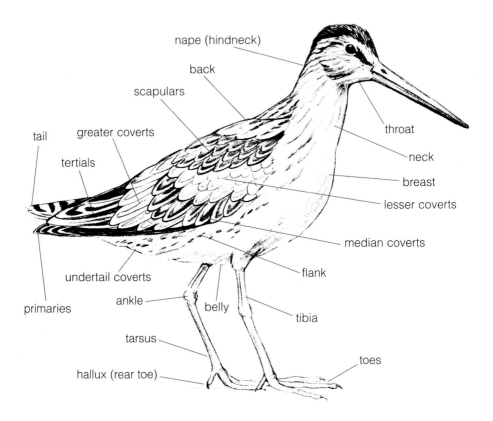

nape (hindneck)

back

scapulars

greater coverts

tail

tertials

throat

neck

breast

lesser coverts

median coverts

undertail coverts

flank

primaries

ankle

belly

tibia

tarsus

hallux (rear toe)

toes

FEATHER PATTERNS

tipped

edged

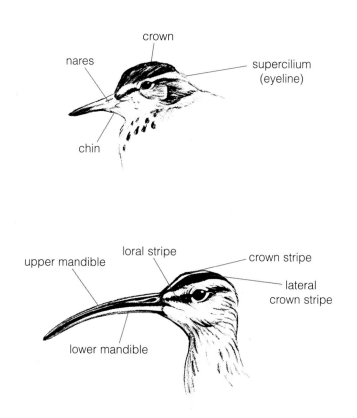

crown

nares

supercilium (eyeline)

chin

loral stripe

upper mandible

crown stripe

lateral crown stripe

lower mandible

fringed

notched

subterminally banded

JULIE ZICKEFOOSE

The plovers, family Charadriidae, all have short, fairly thick bills and relatively short legs. They feed by walking or running several steps, then stopping. Step, step, stop. Step, step, stop. When they stop, they often pick a prey item from the surface.

The great majority of North American shorebird species are in the sandpiper family, Scolopacidae. Varying greatly in size and shape, sandpipers are generally longer-billed and longer-legged than the plovers. And they walk continuously while foraging. Thus, it is usually a fairly simple matter to distinguish between plovers and sandpipers.

Within both larger families there are additional, fairly obvious sub-groupings.

Long-billed Dowitcher in breeding plumage

The plovers fit into one of two sub-groups, the generally smaller, ringed plovers, and the larger, spangled plovers.

Being the largest family, the sandpipers have many more sub-groupings: the godwits, the curlews, the Tringines (yellowlegs and their allies), the turnstones, the phalaropes, the dowitchers, the snipes, the woodcocks, and the largest and most diverse group, the Calidridines (the "typical" sandpipers.)

You will learn to differentiate these sub-groupings using both your field guides and your field experience.

ID ADVICE

Begin by identifying easily recognized species, like those in the avocet and stilt family, both oystercatchers, and Killdeer (make sure to count two neck bands).

Tackle only a few at a time. Learn shorebird anatomy first, and the various feather tracts and individual feather patterns later. Start by sketching one or two distinctive species each day. See and sketch the whole bird and all its features. Try writing descriptions to go with your sketches.

At first, your written descriptions will be crude, but try to include all the basic information: the colors and patterns on the head, neck, breast, belly, and the upperparts, the length, shape, and color of the bill, and the color and length of the legs. Record any behaviors that you witness and describe the call notes that you hear.

After sketching a bird or two, take out your field guide. Identify the bird or birds that you have studied. This will be easy at first when you're working with dissimilar species. When working through shorebird identifications, determining the bird's plumage—breeding, nonbreeding, juvenal, or first winter—is often a prerequisite to identifying the bird as to species. Birds in full breeding plumage, in fresh juvenal plumage, or those completely molted to winter plumage will be

Short-billed Dowitcher in breeding plumage

"aged" easily. But many birds will be molting, that is, changing from one plumage to another, and ageing them will be more difficult at first.

The appearance of every shorebird varies greatly throughout the year because of differences in plumage, molt, feather wear, bleaching by the sun, lighting conditions, the bird's physical condition, its posture, and the manner in which it is holding its feathers (fluffed or retracted).

In some species, there is sexual dimorphism as well—male and female phalaropes, for example, do not look alike. With all this in mind, realize that your sketches and notes will rarely be an exact match for the drawing or photo in your field guide.

American Oystercatcher in breeding plumage

Next, begin working with common species that are not so easily separated. Greater and Lesser Yellowlegs, Western and Least Sandpipers on the Pacific Coast, Least and Semipalmated Sandpipers on the Atlantic, or Wilson's, Piping, and Snowy Plovers on the Gulf Coast, for example.

Sketch the birds, write detailed descriptions, go back to your field guide, and then identify and age the birds. Each species, of course, needs to be studied at different seasons, in different plumages.

Once you are completely familiar with the plumage variations in the most common species, picking out the more uncommon species becomes a snap. Once you come to know what juvenile Semipalmated Sandpipers look like in August, picking out a worn adult White-rumped or a juvenile Baird's will become routine.

As your skills improve, begin working with the more challenging species pairs, like Short-billed and Long-billed Dowitchers. In time, and with practice, you'll find yourself including the colors and patterns of the various feather tracts, and even the colors and patterns of individual feathers.

Now, when you see a bird or a plumage with which you are totally unfamiliar, you'll be able to make a quick sketch and take accurate field notes. In most cases, you'll be able to come up with an acceptable identification. But remember, not all shorebirds, even those that are photographed well, are identifiable.

PLUMAGES AND AGEING

Chapter

2

ow I get it," I said slowly to Tom. "The bird on the right is an *adult*, the one on the left, a *juvenile!*" A smile creased my lips and my eyes must have begun to sparkle. Upon my face was a look of wonder and amazement, a look that I had seen thousands of times as an elementary school teacher in Brooklyn, New York. It was the look that assures the instructor that—in the mind of the student—under-standing has replaced the confusion and uncertainty that reigned only moments before.

Red Knot juvenile

"Tom" was the late Thomas H. Davis, Jr., voice of the New York Rare Bird Alert, field identification expert on two continents, skilled photographer, master shorebirder, and my mentor. It's hard to believe that nearly two decades have passed since I stood in the muck with him at New York City's Jamaica Bay Wildlife Refuge staring through my spotting scope at two Least Sandpipers—one a worn, breeding plumaged adult, the other resplendent in fresh juvenal plumage.

Before that moment, a Least Sandpiper had been—to me—just that, a Least Sandpiper. But Tom's lesson on that hot, humid, mid-August mud flat morning opened up a new world, a world that still—after having carefully observed hundreds of thousands of North American shorebirds—fascinates me immensely.

I soon realized that correctly "ageing" shorebirds, that is, identifying their plumage or "age-class" is, in most cases, easier than identifying them as to species. Some species, like Killdeer and the Long-billed Curlew, however, are difficult to age in the field because their breeding, nonbreeding, and juvenal plumages are so similar.

SHOREBIRD PLUMAGES

Simply put, adult shorebirds have two "suits," or sets of feathers, in their wardrobe: nonbreeding (or winter or basic) plumage, worn for several months on the wintering grounds and at times on southbound or northbound migration; and breeding (or alternate) plumage, worn at times on northbound migration, on the breeding grounds, and at times, on southbound migration.

Birds "change their clothes" by molting; new feathers grow in, pushing out old, worn ones. Many shorebirds molt into breeding plumage during northbound migration and into nonbreeding plumage during southbound migration.

Most species have a distinct nonbreeding plumage in which the feathers of the upperparts are gray or brownish-gray so that the birds will be camouflaged when feeding or roosting on the wet sand beaches or mud flats of the wintering grounds.

Breeding plumage in most species is dramatically different from winter plumage. Strikingly patterned upperparts in various combinations of rich brown and buff, bright orange, silver, gold, black, and white supplant winter's gray garb. Winter's plain white breasts and bellies become streaked, spotted, or heavily barred. In other species these white feathers are replaced by richly colored ones of chestnut or brick red, salmon, red-orange, or jet black. Most of the smaller sandpipers show pure white underparts even in breeding plumage. Handsome adult shorebirds in their fine spring colors are well camouflaged as the earth tones of spring overtake arctic and prairie breeding grounds.

Red Knot in breeding plumage

In the first year, shorebird identification can be a bit more complex. Juvenal plumage, which replaces the natal down sported at birth, is worn for several weeks by some species, such as Wilson's Phalarope, or for several months by most species. It is characterized by warmly colored, evenly patterned upperparts; each feather has distinct buff, white, chestnut, or rufous fringes, tips, or edges, that give the young birds a "crisp" look.

Red Knot in nonbreeding plumage

Young yellowlegs exhibit white notches and/or spots along the edge of each brownish-black feather, and Red Knots show fine, black subterminal bands, but each can still be described as "evenly patterned," and each is easily distinguished from worn adults.

The breasts of the earliest arriving juveniles often have a buffish cast, a glow, that quickly wears to white. Juvenal plumage becomes worn more quickly than adult plumage, the feathers being more fragile. Within weeks, the young-of-the-year lose their bright feather edgings to wear, but they are still easily distinguished by their even patterning.

Juveniles of many species undergo a partial molt en route to the wintering grounds. Juvenal feathers of the back, the scapulars (shoulders), and some or all of the tertials (innermost wing feathers) are replaced by gray winter feathers.

But several rows of worn juvenal coverts (small feathers that protect the folded wing) are retained, their pale fringes still evident. These birds, in first-winter plumage, show gray saddles that contrast with the fringed coverts. The tail and primary and secondary feathers are also retained. Stilt Sandpipers, Red Knots, Dunlins, and Wilson's Phalaropes are commonly seen in first-winter plumage on their southbound migrations.

At about ten months, young shorebirds molt into first-summer plumage, but identification of this age-class in the field is, at best, extremely difficult; some of these birds attain full breeding plumage, others only a partial breeding plumage. Still others wear a set of winter-plumage-like feathers; birds seen May through July that are all-gray above are most likely first-year individuals.

THE TIMING OF MIGRATION

Adult shorebirds of many species, either in, or molting into, breeding plumage, move northward through temperate North American latitudes predominately in April

Least Sandpiper in juvenal plumage

and May. Identification and ageing in spring is relatively straightforward, but molting birds, which show bright breeding feathers interspersed with worn, gray winter feathers, may be somewhat confusing.

Amazingly, the first *southbound* migrant shorebirds—having finished (or failed at) breeding—regularly arrive in the United States during the last week of June. On the West Coast, they arrive even earlier. This is just weeks, even days, after the last *northbound* migrants have departed. (Female Wilson's Phalaropes, however, are already moving south by mid-June; they are occasionally seen side-by-side with late northbound migrants such as White-rumped Sandpipers.)

The appearance of these returning adults varies considerably. Some are still in fairly bright breeding plumage, showing little feather-wear or molt. Others are but pale reminders of their northbound-selves, the bright earth tones of May having faded, abraded, and been bleached by the sun to dishwater browns and grays. By mid-summer, the adults of many species have begun to molt into nonbreeding plumage; the worn, faded breeding feathers are replaced with fresh feathers of winter gray.

In early August, when the wild blackberries of the Northeast are at their sweetest, the first juvenile shorebirds are seen, standing out like jewels, in large flocks of molting adults. On the West Coast, even in Southern California, the first juveniles arrive during the last week of July, considerably earlier than on the East Coast.

When I spot the first juvenile migrant of the season—either a Lesser Yellowlegs or a Least Sandpiper—I never fail to think of Tom Davis. On steamy, muggy afternoons, it seems as if I can hear his voice: "The juveniles have warm colors and even patterns—each feather is neatly fringed. The fading, molting adults are dull with splotchy, irregular patterns."

Tom always carried his full-frame "baby pictures" in a small album that he kept in his shirt pocket, for juvenile shorebirds are—in marked contrast to wary adults—a photographer's delight, often allowing ridiculously close approach.

The juveniles of most migrant species arrive during mid- to late August on the East Coast and about two weeks earlier on the West Coast. In both cases, this is about four to six weeks *after* their parents have arrived. Young White-rumped Sandpipers and Long-billed Dowitchers, however, are not usually seen until mid- to late September in the East and early September in the West. In two species, Dunlin, and American Golden-Plover, the adults and young generally migrate together. The Dunlins show up on the East Coast in mid-September, about two weeks after the first American Golden-Plovers. On the West Coast, adult Pacific Golden-Plovers typically arrive during the third week of July, juveniles regularly in mid- to late August.

This summer—wherever you live—dust off that scope and head for your favorite shorebirding spot. I promise that your first juvenile Least Sandpiper will be a real eye-opener!

B E H A V I O R

Chapter

3

Watching shorebirds do what shorebirds do can be just plain fun. And by closely observing a group of shorebirds for even a short period of time, dozens of interesting behaviors and interactions can be noted.

On several occasions I've witnessed a Short-billed Dowitcher approach a sleeping Hudsonian Godwit from the rear, place its long bill between the godwit's legs, then smartly rap the larger shorebird on the belly. This always causes the godwit to jump about two feet in the

American Golden-Plover juvenile

air and makes me laugh so hard that I nearly fall face-first into the mud.

I've never seen a godwit retaliate. Could this behavior be a form of play (on the dowitcher's part)? No one knows. A bird encyclopedia can be a treasure-trove of behavioral (and other) information, but some of the behaviors that you observe may not be described in comprehensive works nor in the rest of the ornithological literature. It is, therefore, important to observe carefully and keep accurate field notes.

In the early 1980s, while doing a shorebird count in New York City, my friend Arthur Berland and I were startled to see a Willet grab a Least Sandpiper by the neck and pound it into the ground more than two dozen times. After plucking some feathers from the back of the apparently dead little bird, the Willet stood proudly holding the peep in its bill. (The affectionate term "peep" refers to the five small North American sandpipers: Semipalmated, Least, Western, Baird's, and White-rumped.) When the larger bird dropped the Least, the tiny sandpiper ran off into the marsh!

Whimbrel in nonbreeding plumage

Least Sandpiper juvenile

Willets are notorious for their vigorous defense of young and territory, but we didn't know why this one attacked a Least Sandpiper that surely presented no threat at all to its chicks.

G E T T I N G   A R O U N D

Shorebirds get around on the ground by walking or running; nearly all daily activities involve either or both of these forms of locomotion. With the aid of their wings, many shorebirds can jump, often to escape breaking waves or to battle rivals. Shorebirds usually stand on one leg while resting and may hop away on one leg when disturbed; inexperienced observers often mistakenly conclude that these hopping birds are indeed crippled birds with one leg.

While the toes of nearly all shorebird species are perfectly adapted for walking or running, the toes of two species of phalaropes are lobed. These lobed toes help them swim quite well. Other shorebirds, like avocets and yellowlegs, swim fairly well. Still other species, dowitchers and oystercatchers for example, swim occasionally—but rather clumsily.

It has been reported that Spotted Sandpipers dive below the surface while swimming to evade attacking falcons. Many shorebird chicks, which are generally good swimmers, do the same.

F L I G H T

The long, narrow, pointed wings of shorebirds make them superlative fliers. The long-distance migrants are the strongest fliers. The longer, more pointed wings of the golden-plovers, and Pectoral and White-rumped Sandpipers, for example, make them stronger fliers than the short distance (shorter-, broader-winged) migrants, like Spotted Sandpipers and the oystercatchers. Aside from their fabulous migrations, flight—often rapid—is an important part of each shorebird's daily existence. Shorebirds fly to and from their feeding grounds. They fly away from predators, when disturbed while feeding or at their roosts, and—at times—when disturbed at their nests.

Twice at the Jamaica Bay Wildlife Refuge I've seen Peregrine Falcons chasing

individual yellowlegs low over the water after having singled them out of a flock. Both times, when the speeding falcon put on the afterburners and approached to within a yard of its prey, the yellowlegs dove—actually crashed—into the pond. And both times, the falcon could do nothing but continue on.

Shorebirds fly when courting their mates and when defending or advertising their breeding territories; such flights, almost always undertaken by the males, include spectacular displays that often include odd vocalizations not heard elsewhere. And shorebirds may fly above their chicks while guarding them, often fluttering about the tiny balls of fluff.

Shorebirds may fly alone or with ten thousand others. They may fly in species-pure flocks, or in mixed flocks containing a dozen or more species. They may fly with their wingtips grazing the water or at altitudes of four miles or more. They are indeed absolute masters of the air and the wind.

P R E E N I N G

Most shorebirds spend roughly one-tenth of the daylight hours preening, though less time is spent on this activity during the breeding season. Shorebirds

Semipalmated Sandpipers in worn juvenal plumage

often bathe before preening, usually in belly-deep water. Sometimes they submerge themselves up to their necks and remain motionless for a short time. In either case, they tip forward and throw water onto their heads and backs with their bills. Next they beat their wings furiously in place sending spray in all directions.

Some or all of these steps are often repeated several times. Near or at the end of a bath, I have seen many small sandpipers jump into the air while rapidly beating their wings. They always alight nearby, usually in shallower water.

After leaving the water, the wings are whirred again and the feathers are shaken out. Fluffing the feathers allows the bird to get at each individual feather more easily. Feathers are grasped in the bill and pulled through from the base toward the tip—usually one feather at a time. Sometimes the bird nibbles on the feather as this is done. The head and neck feathers are preened by rubbing them against another part of the body or by scratching them with the toes.

Preening removes dirt from the feathers and smoothes the feather barbs so that they lock together tightly. While preening, the bird occasionally rubs its bill on an oil gland located on the rump above the base of its tail. The oil is then worked into the feathers as the bird preens.

ROOSTING

When birds are sleeping, or resting while awake, they are said to be roosting. Shorebirds may roost singly, by the dozen, by the hundreds, or in huge groups numbering in the tens of thousands. Breeding shorebirds often rest or sleep on the nest while incubating.

Migrant shorebirds often roost near their feeding grounds. They may roost on a beach above the high-tide line, on exposed sandbars, on offshore islands, or on rocky outcroppings. At night, many shorebirds prefer to roost in marshes. Some flocks of shorebirds, especially plovers, often choose agricultural areas, grassy fields, or golf courses as places to sleep or rest. This is especially true during or after rainstorms.

Most shorebirds roost with their heads and necks resting on their backs and with their bills tucked neatly into their scapulars. They often sleep standing on two legs or one, but at times, a bird may rest on its tarsi (its lower legs) or lay flat on the ground. When resting, they often keep one or both eyes open slightly—the better to detect incoming falcons with, my dear.

NEST-DISTRACTION DISPLAYS

Many shorebirds, especially the plovers, perform elaborate nest-distraction displays designed to lead predators and human intruders away from the nest and

Black-bellied Plover, nest distraction display

the young. The bird may simply walk away from the nest calling loudly. Or it may leave the nest unseen, jump high into the air, then zigzag away with ruffled feathers, hunched posture, and wings drooped behind. This is called the *rodent run* and is often employed by Purple Sandpiper. The most well known nest distraction displays involves feigning injury. Piping Plovers nestle in the sand with one wing outstretched, as if unable to fly. When approached, they run ahead a short distance and continue the ruse. Killdeer have perfected a variety of broken-wing displays. They hobble pitifully away from the nest dragging both the tail and one wing along the ground. They, too, continue on weakly whenever approached. Eventually, they fly off in perfect form.

AGGRESSIVE BEHAVIORS

Interactions with other creatures, usually birds, are part of the daily lives of shorebirds. Encounters with birds of like species are labeled "intraspecific." Those involving birds of other species are termed "interspecific."

Once I saw a dozen or so southbound juvenile Semipalmated Plovers feeding peacefully along the margin of a brackish impoundment. Suddenly, and for no apparent reason, two birds squared off. They stood completely still and stared at each other for several seconds. Next, one of the birds tipped forward, spread its wings and tail, and gave a shrill call. Finally, it charged the other bird, which tilted forward and stood its ground.

With a few variations thrown in, this intraspecific confrontation continued for several minutes until one of the birds flew about thirty yards away and resumed foraging. As is common with many shorebird species, the young Semi Plovers had been fighting over feeding territory.

Juvenile Sanderling, threat display

Shorebirds routinely defend feeding territories while stopping over during migration and on the wintering grounds. There have even been instances of wintering shorebirds defending the same feeding territory for several successive seasons. During the breeding season, some species do most of their foraging within the pair's aggressively defended breeding territory, while others fly considerable distances to feeding grounds.

Shorebirds often squabble while roosting, fighting at times for the "best" spot. On beaches, this may be a human footprint, where many small plovers prefer to roost. On windy days, many shorebirds roost on the sheltered side of a rock or a piece of driftwood. To get the spot they want, birds may threaten each other with raised wing or other displays, or actually peck at the bird they wish to displace.

One summer, I saw a group of twenty or so small sandpipers and a single Lesser Yellowlegs roosting in very shallow water. All faced into a gentle north breeze. One of the peeps screamed its alarm call and leapt into escape-flight, leading its flockmates toward the north end of the pond. Only the yellowlegs, now facing south, remained.

Juvenile Sanderlings, territorial battle

As I glanced over my right shoulder to discover the cause of the birds' distress, a Merlin sliced through the still, muggy morning toward the remaining shorebird. "Yellowlegs lunch," I imagined, and so—I'm sure—did the small, powerful falcon. But the slim young bird stood its ground, leaned forward, and raised its wings in defiance. To my amazement (and possibly to the yellowlegs' amazement as well), the dark falcon veered off in search of more cooperative prey.

I reached for my field notebook and pen, and made note of yet another of the remarkable interspecific clashes that add spice to the shorebirding stew.

FEEDING AND DIET

Chapter

4

S horebirds exhibit a great variety of feeding behaviors. Some feed in the same manner all year-round. Others vary their approach as the seasons, locales, and food items change.

Many shorebirds, especially the plovers, pick their food from the surface after first locating it visually; their large eyes are evolutionary adaptations. Most sandpipers either pick food from the surface or probe into soft mud or sand while foraging.

Probing involves shorebirds using their soft, sensitive bill tips to feel

Preceding pages: Black-bellied Plover pulling marine worm

for the various invertebrates that make up the bulk of their diet. The tips of many shorebird bills are also flexible—they can be used to extract prey items such as marine worms or the larvae of aquatic insects from their burrows.

Long-billed Dowitcher juvenile

If all the birds in a mixed flock of feeding shorebirds had bills of the same length, the mud flat prey items at a single depth would be rapidly depleted. But there is great variation in bill length among shorebirds. This allows many different species to feed on the same flat without depleting the food resources.

On all U.S. and southern Canadian coasts, Semipalmated Plovers, Semipalmated and Western Sandpipers, Short-billed Dowitchers, Lesser

Yellowlegs, and Dunlins are often seen feeding together on tidal flats. The Semi Plovers, with their short bills, feed on the driest portions of the flats, picking prey items from the surface. The Semi Sandpipers feed on the wet mud, either picking prey from the surface or probing just a fraction of an inch into the mud.

The Westerns and Dunlins, with their longer decurved bills, usually feed in shallow water, probing into the soft mud below for food. Dunlins, the larger of the two species, often feed in deeper water than Western Sandpipers. And because the Dunlin's bill is a bit longer as well, the two birds utilize different food resources.

The dowitchers, with their long, straight bills, probe deeply and repeatedly into soft mud with a sewing-machine-like motion while foraging in the shallows. The yellowlegs also wade the shallows, capturing mostly aquatic insect prey directly from the water with their thin, pointed bills.

Differences in shorebird leg lengths also ensures that food resources at a single substrate level will not be depleted by mixed-species shorebird flocks feeding on the same flat. The Dunlin and the Stilt Sandpiper are roughly the same size and their bills are similarly shaped. The Dunlin, however, is considerably shorter-legged, so the Stilt Sandpiper is able to feed in deeper water and utilize different food resources, even when the birds are foraging within yards of each other.

Several species of shorebirds are extremely specialized feeders. American Avocets, while walking or rushing forward (often in groups as large as several hundred), capture their prey by swishing their slim, upcurved bills just below the water's surface. (Greater Yellowlegs often feed in a similar manner.) The avocet's close relative, the Black-necked Stilt, uses its straight, needlelike bill primarily to capture insects.

Oystercatchers insert their laterally flattened bills into partially-opened bivalves to cut the adductor muscle, much like a fisherman using a clam knife. If the bivalve is tightly closed, these large birds use their bills as hammers to smash a hole in the shell and then cut the adductor muscle. In either case, the soft meat is easily extracted and eaten. The bill may first be used as a crowbar to pry mollusks from rocks.

Both American Woodcocks and Common Snipes have long, straight bills that they plunge deeply and repeatedly into soft earth while feeling for prey with their soft, sensitive bill tips. Their upper mandibles are flexible so that the bill tip can be opened to seize their favorite prey items: earthworms. Woodcocks—which reportedly stamp their feet to stir the earthworms—have been known to eat their weight in these delectable morsels in less than a day!

Turnstones are named for their habit of lifting stones, pebbles, and empty shells with their bills to search for prey items below. All shorebirds have diets that include a vast variety of food items, and the turnstone diet probably leads the list.

Turnstones consume bivalves, limpets, barnacles, snails, sand "fleas" (amphipods), marine worms, shrimps and prawns, sea slugs, horseshoe crab eggs, a great variety of insects and insect larvae (including adult and larval midges, grasshoppers, and flesh fly grubs), carrion (especially rotting fish), spiders, small crabs, seeds, berries, and tern eggs. At Daytona Beach, Florida, I have seen Ruddy Turnstones foraging just inches from the feet of food-cart patrons. Here they dine on popcorn, bits of frankfurters, and french fries with ketchup.

Shorebird diets change with the seasons and with the birds' choice of habitats. During the breeding season in the Far North many species ingest plant matter for sustenance, eating seeds early in the season and relying on berries after the insect population has declined. When insects abound, however, they are the main prey items for most shorebird species on both prairie and arctic breeding grounds.

The peak of chick hatching almost always coincides with periods of great insect abundance; adult and larval insects make up the bulk of most species' diets at this time. (Adult insects are captured primarily by pecking and picking, but larvae and grubs can be captured by probing.) On migration and on the wintering grounds many species prefer small crustaceans, mollusks, and marine worms.

MATING AND BREEDING

Chapter

5

I n June 1995, I had the pleasure of visiting the prairies and meadows of central Montana and the subarctic tundra of Churchill, Manitoba.

In Montana, Marbled Godwits executed spectacular display flights above the yellowed prairie grasses. American Avocets walked across alkali flats in stately fashion to take over incubating duties from their mates. And twice I witnessed female-female mounting by Wilson's Phalaropes.

Churchill was even more exciting. Male Hudsonian Godwits, their breasts and bellies the color of fresh bricks, stood guard over their mates on hillocks covered with tiny purple rosebay flowers. Swimming male Red-necked Phalaropes crouched submissively when approached by stunningly gorgeous females. And Lesser Yellowlegs gave raised-wing displays from atop stunted spruce trees.

Lesser Yellowlegs in breeding plumage

Dunlins approached their well concealed nests by crawling through grassy tunnels like mice. Stilt Sandpipers sat steadfastly on their four-egg clutches. And a female American Golden-Plover led an intruder from its nest by stumbling pitifully across moss-covered hillocks pretending to have a broken wing. What a thrill it was to see for myself the breeding behaviors that I had read about for years.

DEFENDING TERRITORIES

For a given species, the breeding season begins with the arrival of the first birds on their breeding grounds. In some species, the males (which often arrive first) stake out territories. In others, the males first select a mate and then the pair defends the nesting territory together. Neither male nor female phalaropes defend a territory, but the females will, at times, defend their males from other females.

The breeding territories defended by the males of some species, like Pectoral and White-rumped Sandpipers, are reported to be little more than mating areas—all females that enter these large, often overlapping territories are courted. As the season progresses, males often display to females near their nests, but these efforts are almost always rebuffed.

At times, shorebirds may arrive on the breeding grounds already paired. This may be the result of pair bonding that has taken place en route, or may simply be the result of a bird reuniting with its mate from the previous breeding season.

MATING SYSTEMS

Shorebirds employ as wide a variety of mating systems as any other group of birds. Many species, like Western, Baird's, Least, Semipalmated, Purple, Solitary, and Stilt Sandpipers, both dowitchers, both godwits, both yellowlegs, Wandering Tattler, Killdeer, the spangled plovers, Whimbrel, Long-billed Curlew, American Avocet, and Black Oystercatcher, are all thought to be strictly monogamous.

Pairs of Black Oystercatchers stay together year-round and may nest in the same spot, with the same mate, for years, while Baird's Sandpipers almost always switch mates annually. In most monogamous pairings both sexes share the incubation chores, but fewer species also share the task of tending the young.

In Long-billed and Short-billed Dowitchers, and Purple and Stilt Sandpipers, for example, both sexes incubate, but the female deserts soon after hatching, leaving only the male to care for the brood. In Whimbrels, and Least and Semipalmated Sandpipers, however, both sexes incubate and tend the young until they are fledged (able to fly).

Under most conditions, Snowy Plovers are monogamous. In California, however, where females often greatly outnumber males, the female Snowys often desert their mates after hatching and re-nest with another male. This is called polyandry—having more than one male mate. And rarely, after the chicks have fledged, the males may re-nest with a different female. This is termed polygyny—having more than one female mate.

In both cases, these polygamous behaviors are termed sequential, since the birds mate with one bird first, and then with another. There are also documented instances of sequential polyandry in Piping and Mountain Plovers, with the females leaving after hatching to re-nest with another male.

Buff-breasted Sandpiper male in single-wing display

In Spotted Sandpipers (and several other shorebird species) the sex roles are reversed. The females have larger and blacker spots than males. The females arrive first on the breeding grounds and select and defend territories. And it is the females who aggressively court the males. The males incubate the eggs and tend the young.

Many sex-role-reversed shorebirds are polyandrous, and researchers have shown that older female Spotted Sandpipers often engage in sequential polyandry. At times, though, they take things even further, laying four-egg clutches for two males at once. This is termed simultaneous polyandry.

In the three North American phalarope species the sex roles are also reversed. The female phalaropes are larger and more brightly colored than the males, and it is the females that pursue, court, and defend the males. (The females do not defend territories, but rather follow and defend the males from approach by other females.) It is the male phalarope that builds the nest, develops a brood patch—the bare skin on a bird's belly that is used to warm the eggs—and cares for the chicks.

Red Phalarope female in breeding plumage

Many phalarope pairs are monogamous, but some female phalaropes engage in sequential polyandry, abandoning the male after the clutch is complete and pursuing, courting, and mating with another male—and sometimes, in the same season, with a third!

Male Pectoral and male White-rumped Sandpipers are typically polygynous. Males of these species may stay with a female until the clutch of eggs is complete and then mate again with another female. Or they may copulate with and fertilize several females within a one week period.

Buff-breasted Sandpiper male in embrace display

Of the shorebird species that breed regularly in North America, the Buff-breasted Sandpiper is the only one to use a "lek." Between two and ten males typically gather on display areas known as leks, which offer no resources at all for the females—they are simply sites where males can show off to prospective mates. The leks are quite large and each of the males defends a territory on the lek against other males.

At least seventeen complex and distinctly different male courtship displays have been noted in the Buff-breasted Sandpiper. Most involve the raising and waving of one or both wings—the white wing linings appear to flash during these wing-up displays, as they do during flutter-jump displays. In the spectacular double-wing display the male holds its arched wings as if to embrace the females, which approach closely and appear to inspect the male's under-wing linings. Mounting occurs after the closest female turns her back to the male and opens her wings. Males from adjacent territories occasionally disrupt both courtship displays and imminent copulations.

TERRITORIES

Breeding territories are defended and advertised in a number of ways. Ground displays may include calls. Aerial displays may include calls or songs. Boundaries may be patrolled either in flight or by walking. And intruders—usually of the same species—may be charged, chased, and physically attacked.

Ground displays usually consist of a series of behaviors, each increasing in

American Oystercatcher in piping display

intensity. First, the bird may simply stand tall, retract its feathers, and stare. Then, it may pull in its neck and crouch in a low, horizontal position. Some species then threaten by raising one or both wings, exposing the wing linings.

If these displays fail to drive off an intruder, the bird may tip forward, spread its tail feathers, and give a loud, trill call. Sometimes the wings are vibrated during this maneuver. Finally, the territorial bird—with wings held low—may charge at the intruder and attempt to peck at it. If the interloper flies away, the defender may pursue it to ensure that it is driven completely out of the territory.

Other species try different tacks. Oystercatchers defend with a piping display: with heads down and necks arched they call shrilly and repeatedly. The piping display also serves as a greeting between mates and may help solidify the pair bond (as may the territorial defenses of other species, as well).

Black-necked Stilts hover above intruders with their heads down and their legs dangling, while screaming their *"kik kik kik"* calls.

Killdeer may stand at the edge of their territory calling *"di-yit"* every few seconds for as long as several hours. Ruddy Turnstones choose elevated perches from which to display. They crouch, vibrate their tails, and make a strange clicking noise. Both types of displays serve not only to proclaim territory but to advertise for a mate as well.

Snowy Plovers often run at intruders and then battle breast to breast, wings flailing, as the birds jab at and push each other. Male Western Sandpipers also engage in a great deal of fighting while defending their territories. They often flutter several feet into the air, clawing at their rivals with their toes and striking them with their wings.

DISPLAY FLIGHTS

Many shorebird species perform spectacular display flights. In some species, they are performed only by the male. Among the species where both sexes perform display flights are Semipalmated Plover, Long-billed Dowitcher, American Golden-Plover, Dunlin, and Baird's, Semipalmated, and Stilt Sandpipers. Female Spotted Sandpipers fly display flights alone.

These display flights serve two purposes. They proclaim territorial ownership and advertise the bird's presence to potential mates nearby. In many cases, they may constitute the beginning of pair bonding as well.

The height and extent of these territorial display flights varies tremendously. Male Pectoral Sandpipers display while flying slowly just a few feet above the tundra, but they may fly distances of 400 or 500 feet. Semipalmated Sandpipers fly 25 to 50 feet above tundra, but their flights are generally restricted to the area surrounding the nest.

Pectoral Sandpiper male

American Golden-Plovers may display any-where from 25 to several hundred feet in the air, and Hudsonian Godwits may spiral as high as 800 feet. Both of these species may fly 1/4 to 1/2 mile from the spot where the flight originated. Wandering Tattlers reach heights of 1,000 feet and may travel as far as a mile to let adjacent pairs know of their presence.

The patterns and flight styles vary as well. Some species fly figure-eights, some great cir-cles. Some angle upward at a forty-five-degree angle, others reach maximum height by flying a switchback pattern, and still others rise almost perpendicularly. Some fly slowly, while others streak across the northern skies.

Some beat their wings deeply, some shallowly; some flutter, some glide. Others beat their arched wings stiffly; still others vibrate them rapidly. Many shorebirds, including Long-billed Dowitchers and Dunlins, hover on quivering wings. American Golden-Plovers fly—like Common Nighthawks—with raised wings that barely beat below the horizontal and exaggerat-ed upstrokes, repeatedly calling *"chu-leet, chu-leet."*

Some shorebirds descend slowly in a glide, some parachute down on raised wings. Others fold their wings and drop to the earth like rocks, raising their wings at the last instant so as to land softly while displaying.

Most species call during display flights. Some calls are similar to the calls commonly heard while the birds are on migration or on the wintering grounds. But others are, well, other-worldly. Male Pectorals inflate their chests and utter eerie *"whoops"* every few seconds; these calls peak in volume as the male flies over the female. Lesser Yellowlegs pairs fly together yodeling *"pill-e-wee, pill-e-wee."* Female Wilson's Phalaropes bark like dogs and Sanderlings croak like frogs.

At dusk, Woodcocks *"peent"* nasally, produce a twittering trill with their wingtips as they ascend, and a bubbling warble as they descend. Snipes "win-now" by vibrating their tail feathers as they dive.

And the call of a displaying Short-billed Dowitcher is a musical liquid gurgle; when I first heard it in Churchill, I was stunned. Could that noise have come from a *bird*?

PAIR BONDING

In addition to display flights, there are several other types of pair bonding behaviors. A good number of these behaviors are used by many shorebird species; a few are species-specific.

American and Pacific Golden-Plovers, Black-bellied Plovers, Sanderlings, Common Snipes, and Pectoral Sandpipers, among others, perform complex ground displays that feature the male cocking and/or spreading the tail feathers. In some species the body is held horizontally; in others, the head is lowered as the tail is raised.

Shrill calls or twittering whistles are often part of these displays. Male Pectorals utter a deep vibrato hooting. During these displays, a shorebird's wings may be held tightly against the sides, drooped, or spread to the side and either held still or vibrated rapidly.

Woodcocks raise their wings and hold them overhead as part of the tail-spreading display. Male White-rumped Sandpipers lower their heads, expose

Spotted Sandpiper female displaying

their white rumps, hold their wings out to the side and scurry about in front of the female while making buzzing noises.

Male Dunlins, and Purple, Least, Semipalmated, and many other sandpipers raise a single wing while displaying to their mates. The female Spotted Sandpiper raises both wings, her head, and her tail as she struts around in front of the male. The male Willet walks toward the female while waving both wings high overhead and loudly calling *"dik, dik, dik."*

These ground displays are, at times, performed on northbound migration. At Great Kills National Recreation Area, on Staten Island, New York, I once marveled at the sight of a handsome male Black-bellied Plover displaying while facing *away* from the female. He tilted forward and spread his tail right in her face. She was obviously impressed as she stood transfixed for more than a minute each time that he displayed.

Nest-scraping displays are an important part of pair bonding for Killdeer, Mountain, Semipalmated, and Piping Plovers, Western, Spotted and Stilt Sandpipers, and several other North American species. A typical display begins with the male rotating his breast while pressing it into the ground or into a tundra depression and kicking out dirt or sand with his feet. He may then tip forward, spread his wings, cock his tail, and call. In some species, the female walks up behind the male and either stands closely behind or enters the scrape after he departs. Many depressions may be made before the pair bond is cemented and a single scrape is selected as the nest site. Side-by-side neck preening may take place after nest-scraping displays.

Both aerial and ground chases play an important role in mate selection and pair bonding. In most species, it is the male that chases the female, either by running or by flying. During ground chases, the males often perform a variety of other ground displays. In flight, the males of several sandpiper species overtake the females, fly just ahead of them, and hold their wings in a V while rocking from side to side and calling. And one or more female phalaropes often pursue males that take flight.

In Churchill, I witnessed the aerial chases of American Golden-Plovers and Hudsonian Godwits. The godwit chases were the more spectacular of the two as these large shorebirds are extremely fast, agile fliers. Oftentimes there would be two males zig-zagging high above the tundra pursuing a single female.

COPULATION

Many of the displays and pair bonding behaviors serve as precopulatory displays as well, especially the ground displays and chases. The females of some species invite copulation by leaning forward with their chin held just above the ground or water, often holding this horizontal position for several minutes. The male may or may not accept the invitation. If the former, he may climb or jump onto the back of the female, often with the aid of raised wings. The wings are then flapped in place to maintain balance. The male may rub his breast against the female's back or grasp the back of her neck with his bill while copulating.

Wilson's Phalaropes in precopulatory stand

Researchers in Minnesota recently discovered that female Spotted Sandpipers may store the sperm of older males for up to a month. The eggs fertilized by the stored sperm are laid in the nests of younger, inexperienced males who then incubate till hatching and tend the young!

E G G S   A N D   Y O U N G

Chapter

6

ontained in the egg of a shorebird are the miracles of life and flight. From a tiny embryo grows a feathered creature able to cross continents at two months of age.

Development within the egg is rapid; three to four weeks after fertilization takes place a tiny, helpless, wet bird with only stubs for wings emerges from its shell. Within hours, a baby shorebird is capable of leaving the nest and feeding itself. In a month or so, the once downy newborn is fully grown, fully feathered and able to fly.

EGGS

Most shorebird species lay four eggs, but for some, three is the norm. Late season clutches may contain only one or two eggs. Clutches are generally completed in four to seven days. Shorebird eggs are relatively large.

Most shorebirds lay pear-shaped (pyriform) eggs that are pointed at one end. The pointed ends meet at the center of the nest so that the eggs are neatly packed; this conserves heat and makes it easier for the adult to incubate the eggs.

The base color of shorebird eggs is often green, ranging from pale-green to dark-olive. Or it may be whitish, gray, cream, buff, tan, or brown. The eggs are always blotched, mottled, streaked, spotted, or speckled blackish, dark brown, reddish-brown or purple.

Larger females tend to lay larger eggs than smaller females of the same species, and there is some variation in the size and weight of eggs in a single clutch as well. American Oystercatchers generally lay either two or three eggs, with the second always the largest. Incubation begins when the second egg is laid, therefore the second egg is more likely to survive till fledging than either the first egg (which is smaller) or the third egg (which may be abandoned after the first two eggs hatch synchronously).

Other threats to egg survival abound. Many shorebird eggs are eaten by gulls and jaegers, or by foxes, weasels and other small mammals. Some nests are inadvertently trampled by humans. Cows and horses occasionally step on the eggs of Killdeer and Upland Sandpipers.

INCUBATION AND HATCHING

Small sandpipers, like Westerns and Leasts, incubate their eggs between 19 and 22 days. Medium-sized species, like Red Knots and Greater Yellowlegs, incubate the eggs for 23 to 25 days. The small and medium-sized plovers incubate for a day or two longer, on average, than similarly sized sandpipers. The larger shorebirds, incubate between 26 and 32 days.

Some shorebirds begin incubating before the clutch is complete. In these cases hatching may occur over a period as long as one to two days. When incubation is begun only after the clutch is complete, hatching is fairly synchronous—all the eggs hatch within an hour or two.

From one to three days before it hatches, a baby shorebird uses its egg tooth (a small, horny tubercle near the tip of the upper mandible) to make a tiny, star-shaped hole in the large end of the egg. This process is called pipping.

Alternately struggling and resting, the chick enlarges the hole and turns within the egg, making additional openings until it is able to crack the egg in two using its bill and its head, finally emerging completely from the shell. The adult tending the nest never helps with hatching, but almost always removes the broken pieces of shell from the vicinity of the nest.

CHICKS

The young of many birds are *altricial*, hatched helpless, naked, and blind. They are wholly dependent on their parents for food and care for at least the first several weeks of their lives. Young shorebirds, on the other hand, are *precocial*. When they hatch, they are just about ready to get up and go. Wet at the time of hatching, most remain in the nest for from 1 to 12 hours to dry off and recover from the ordeal of hatching, but most are able to walk from the nest and begin pecking at food within three hours.

Wilson's Phalarope chicks leave the nest immediately after hatching and begin feeding, and they are able to swim within one hour. Western Sandpiper young have better manners—they remain in the nest until the last egg is hatched.

American Golden-Plover Chick

Shorebird chicks are, well, there's no other way to say it, extremely cute. They are covered with natal down, a protective coat of fuzzy feathers. The down is colored and patterned so that it roughly matches the bird's background, making it difficult for predators to locate the young by sight.

Black-necked Stilt chick

The ground color of the down on the upperparts may be gray, golden-yellow, yellow-buff, rust, cream, brown, or reddish-brown. Most chicks are striped, barred, mottled, speckled, or spotted black, dark brown, rust, or yellow-buff, but some are dark overall above. The underparts are usually the same color as the upperparts, but in some species, the underparts are white. Chins, faces and hindneck patches may be white as well.

Shorebird young generally begin pecking at prey items as soon they leave the nest; most—but not all—are able to capture and eat the objects of their attention. Black Oystercatcher chicks, for example, can walk and swim well within three days of hatching, but cannot feed themselves until the fifth day. Not to worry—adults of this species feed the chicks, at times continuing until long after the chicks have fledged.

At least one of the parent shorebirds stays with the chicks between one and many weeks to care for the young. The parents signal danger by giving their alarm call. The well-camouflaged chicks respond by freezing in place and remaining motionless. Young Snowy Plovers flatten themselves in the sand.

Piping Plover chick

The chicks need to be brooded by the adults for several days to a week after hatching. This practice serves both to keep them warm and to protect them. Some species, especially those where only one sex tends the young, brood intermittently. When both sexes offer care, chicks at the nest may be brooded constantly for a week or more. During inclement weather, older chicks are often brooded as well.

In spite of excellent camouflage and good parental care, shorebird chick mortality is extremely high, due to predation, starvation, exposure to the elements and disease. Certainly, more perish than survive. But many are able to keep warm, find food, avoid predation, grow their juvenal feathers, and fledge successfully.

When the chick is between four days and a week old, juvenal feathers begin pushing their way through the skin of the various feather tracts. As this happens, down can often be seen on the tips of the new feathers, giving the young birds a comical look during this stage.

The molt to juvenal plumage is usually complete in ten days to five weeks—the smaller the bird, the faster the feathers grow in. In two to six weeks the young shorebirds are able to fly strongly. By this time, all the adult sandpipers and plovers have abandoned their young.

The young of most migratory species are now completely on their own. They need to feed heavily for several weeks more, after which they will depart for their wintering grounds. Many will fly—unescorted by adults—to southern South America. The miracles of the shorebird year are complete, the cycle ready to begin anew.

M I G R A T I O N

Chapter

7

uring the third week of May 1985, on my first visit to Villas, in Cape May County, New Jersey, I crossed the dune at the west end of town precisely at high tide. I had been assured that many thousands of Ruddy Turnstones, Sanderlings, and Red Knots would be gathered on the fifteen-yard-wide beach to dine on the eggs of the horseshoe crab. But stare as I might, only an empty gravel beach appeared before me. Without warning or apparent cause, the entire "beach" lifted off and took flight: roughly 60,000 Ruddy Turnstones, 30,000 Sanderlings,

Marbled Godwit

and 10,000 Red Knots formed a huge dark cloud, swept out briefly over Delaware Bay, then quickly resettled, once again darkening the beach.

S T A G I N G   A R E A S

Migrant shorebirds routinely fly great distances without stopping for food or rest. Between these flights, huge numbers of tired, hungry sandpipers and plovers gather for several days to two weeks at exceedingly food-rich areas. The birds are dependent on these critical stopover sites—called staging areas. By feeding ravenously, the birds are able to deposit layers of fat on their breasts. This fat fuels the next leg of their migratory journey.

In North America, eight major staging areas are well-known to shorebird biologists. The Copper River Delta in Alaska, Gray's Harbor in southwestern Washington state, the wetlands surrounding San Francisco Bay, Great Salt Lake in Utah, the Lahontan Valley (or Carson Sink) in Nevada, Cheyenne Bottoms in Kansas, the Bay of Fundy (between New Brunswick and Nova Scotia, Canada), and the Delaware Bay shore (Delaware and New Jersey) all attract 500,000 to several million or more shorebirds during each calendar year.

The attractiveness of a staging area is entirely dependent on the food resources available at a given time. Sites that offer a wealth of invertebrate prey items during both spring and fall migration periods are utilized by both northbound and southbound migrants, but such sites are the exception, rather than the rule.

Corophium volutator is an obscure, mud-dwelling amphipod. Every August, as many as 350,000 southbound migrant Semipalmated Sandpipers and thousands of other shorebirds stop at Mary's Point, New Brunswick, on the Bay of Fundy to feed on uncountable numbers of this single invertebrate species. And there are plenty enough to go around—shorebird migrations are timed to coincide with periods of peak prey abundance.

The vast majority of Semipalms, adequately refueled and spurred on by northwest winds, depart en masse on a cool, clear early evening. Their next stop? For many, it is the northern coast of South America in Suriname or French Guiana, 2,400 miles to the southeast. Their non-stop flight over the Atlantic takes roughly forty hours.

After leaving their interior northwestern breeding grounds, huge numbers of Wilson's Phalaropes stage at several key locations, the two most important being Great Salt Lake, Utah (600,000 birds), and Mono Lake, California (80,000 birds). The menu at both sites is the same: brine shrimp and brine flies.

The energy provided by the tiny invertebrate prey allows adult birds of this species to begin and complete their molt to nonbreeding plumage while at the staging areas. Most of these phalaropes double their body weight during stays of

Red Knot flock

six to eight weeks. Some become so fat that just before leaving for South America they are too heavy to fly and can be caught by hand!

SPRING MIGRATION

Each spring in March and April, untold numbers of shorebirds leave their wintering grounds in southern North America, Central America, and South America and undertake long migratory flights, stopping every few hundred, possibly even every few thousand miles, to refuel at food-rich estuaries.

Banding and radar studies have shown that long-distance migrant shorebirds routinely fly nonstop for forty to eighty hours at speeds well in excess of forty miles per hour and at altitudes of approximately 18,000 feet. A Red Knot, color-banded by researchers in southeastern Brazil, was recaptured thirteen days later in New Jersey, 5,500 miles to the north!

Northbound spring migration is a hurried affair. Many individuals travel from South America to their breeding grounds in approximately two months. The birds are spurred on by a migratory urge that German ornithologists term *zugunruhe*. This urge is hormonally controlled; hormones also control the bird's ability to accumulate fat stores easily. By late May or June, most of these millions of shorebirds have made their way to their breeding grounds, usually on northern prairies or arctic or subarctic tundra.

Studies show that male Western Sandpipers winter farther north than females, thus they arrive on the breeding grounds from several days to a week before their mates. This gives them time to occupy and defend territories. The Spotted Sandpiper's sex roles are reversed—the females are first to arrive on the breeding grounds to occupy and defend territories.

FALL MIGRATION

When finished breeding (or having given up entirely) in late June or early July, adult shorebirds of many species form large flocks, often at food-rich river

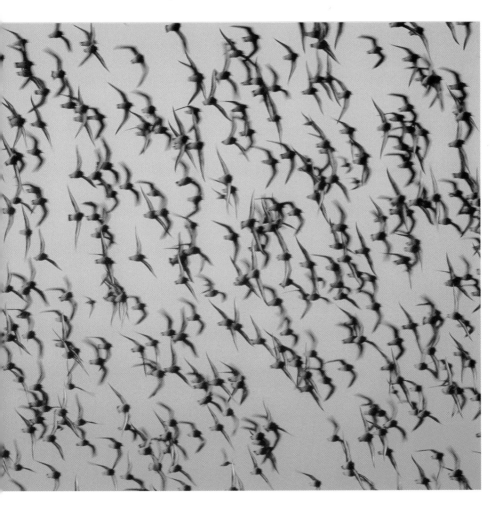

deltas, and feed heavily, fattening themselves for the trip south to wintering grounds in the southern United States, the Caribbean, and Central and South America. Some regularly reach extreme southern South America. For shorebirds, "fall" migration begins in late June and continues at least through November.

In species where the males have the primary responsibility for care of the young, the females migrate first. In species where the females tend the young, the males precede them on migration.

During late June and throughout July, the juvenile shorebirds—though fully feathered and able to fly—are left behind as the adults begin their southbound migration. The young birds need to feed for several weeks to lay fat on their breasts, just as their parents do. The deposited fat provides energy for their first flight south. Most young-of-the-year leave the breeding grounds three to six weeks after their parents have departed.

Southbound migration is a much more leisurely affair than northbound migration. Some species take four months or more to make their way to the wintering grounds. Migratory flights are often just short hops, and many species head south over much broader fronts than in spring.

Juveniles, obviously on their first trip south, are especially likely to wander. Adult Buff-breasted Sandpipers, for example, stick strictly to the interior in spring, but in fall, some young birds make it to coastal areas, much to the delight of shorebirders.

Black Oystercatcher in nonbreeding plumage

Several species—including Baird's and White-rumped Sandpipers and the golden-plovers—routinely make annual round trips in excess of 20,000 miles. Pectoral Sandpipers, however, may make the longest migratory flights of *all* birds, including the fabled Arctic Tern, some Pectorals, which winter in southern South America, breed as far west as central Siberia!

Snowy Plovers and both oystercatcher species, however, are short distance migrants. Most move south no more than a few hundred miles, though some travel more than 700 miles along the coast from southern Oregon to southern California. (Some Snowy Plovers in California actually winter to the *north* of their breeding grounds!) Several populations of these and other shorebird species, such as American and Black Oystercatchers, do not migrate at all—they nest and winter in the same area.

Many shorebird species use the same routes on both northbound and southbound migration. Among these are Purple Sandpipers, Short-billed Dowitchers, Surfbirds, Greater Yellowlegs, and both turnstones.

On the other hand, Least and White-rumped Sandpipers, some populations of Semipalmated Sandpipers, Hudsonian Godwits, and American Golden-Plovers—among others—usually exhibit elliptical migratory patterns. Fall migration is largely transoceanic—the birds depart the Maritime Provinces and New England and fly south and east over the Atlantic to South America. In spring, they migrate through Central America and up the center of North America to the breeding grounds.

S P E C I E S

T he following species accounts are arranged in American Ornithologists
Union (AOU) order. The AOU publishes a checklist of the birds of North
America; it is revised every few years. The birds are listed in taxonomic
order next to their closest relatives—those most similar genetically.

The accounts give a general overview of each species' natural
history including its general appearance and structure, its migratory

Western Sandpipers in breeding plumage

ACCOUNTS

patterns, the location of its breeding and wintering areas, its preferred seasonal habitats, its diet, and the structure and placement of its nest.

While the species accounts are not intended to provide a feather by feather description of each bird in each plumage, I have attempted to boil down my nearly two decades of experience into a thick soup containing the meat and potatoes of shorebird ageing and identification.

B L A C K - B E L L I E D   P L O V E R
(*Pluvialis squatarola*)

This bulky, short-necked species is North America's largest plover. In the last century it was saved from being slaughtered by market hunters by its wariness and by its habit of traveling in smaller flocks than did golden-plovers.

Known as Grey Plover in Europe, this species breeds on Arctic tundra worldwide. The eggs are laid in a scratched-out hollow lined with dried grasses and moss.

Quite striking in breeding dress, they are spangled silver, black, and white above and are black from face to belly with white undertail coverts. They have a grayish crown, and a broad white stripe outlining the face and extending down the sides to the lower breast. Spring males are more solidly black below and are slightly larger than their mates. Females are brownish-black and mottled whitish below.

This common species picks crustaceans and marine worms from wet sand and mud flats with its short, stubby, black bill. (The bill of the golden-plover is smaller and slimmer.) When frequenting fields and wet meadows, Black-bellieds feed mainly on grasshoppers, beetles, grubs, and earthworms.

Adults head south in July and August and winter on U.S., Central American, and all but southern South American coasts. In nonbreeding plumage, they are rather plain; the feathers of the upperparts are brownish-gray, spotted, notched, and fringed whitish; below they are white with grayish streaks. In all plumages, the legs of Black-bellied Plovers are black or dark gray.

Black-bellied Plovers in fresh juvenal plumage can be confused with juvenile American Golden-Plovers because they are both spotted golden-buff above. Young Black-bellieds, however, are *streaked* on the neck, breast, and belly; young Goldens are *barred* in these areas.

On the rear flanks, juvenile Black-bellieds are almost always white and unstreaked, whereas juvenile American Golden-Plovers are barred on a buff background. In all plumages, the white rump and black axillary ("armpit") feathers of Black-bellied Plovers as seen in flight are diagnostic.

For me, no walk along the coast at any season is complete without hearing the plaintive, whistled *"peee-oooo-eeee"* of a fly-by Black-bellied Plover.

Black-bellied Plover juvenile

AMERICAN GOLDEN-PLOVER
(*Pluvialis Dominicus*)

Smaller, more slender and elegant, and proportionately smaller-headed than the closely related Black-bellied Plover, the American Golden-Plover has recently been split from the nearly identical Pacific Golden-Plover. Scientists formerly considered these two birds races of the same species: the Lesser Golden-Plover.

In all plumages, American Golden-Plovers in flight are easily distinguished from Black-bellieds by their uniformly dark upperparts and grayish underwing and axillary feathers.

In full breeding plumage the American Golden-Plover is breathtakingly beautiful. Gold spangled upperparts extend to the nape and crown. They are black from the face through the undertail coverts with a white stripe down the sides to the lower breast as in breeding Black-bellied Plovers. The males are more solidly

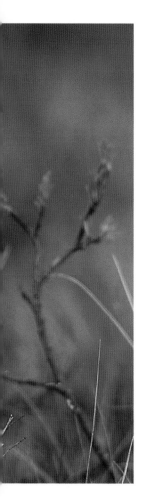

American Golden-Plover male in breeding plumage

black below than females. The bill is black, and the legs blackish, as they are year-round.

American Golden-Plovers breed on well-drained Arctic tundra in northern Canada and Alaska. The nest is a simple depression lined with lichens and mosses.

Juveniles are seen on migration from coast to coast from late August to early November. They are distinguished from juvenile Black-bellies by their darker caps and more distinct eyelines as well as by previously mentioned differences in both structure and in the patterning of the upperparts (as seen when the birds are in flight.)

In nonbreeding plumage, American Golden-Plovers are brownish-gray above, the feathers fringed or notched dull gold or whitish. The breasts are gray, the bellies whitish. Many migrate non-stop over the western Atlantic from eastern Canada and the northeastern United States to Brazil and then to the wintering grounds on the Argentine pampas. Northbound migration is primarily inland all the way from Argentina to the Arctic. Migrants of this species generally prefer plowed fields, flooded rice fields, pastures, and other short-grass habitats where they feed primarily on grasshoppers, crickets, and grubs. They are strong, swift fliers, deservedly well-known as champion long-distance migrants.

PACIFIC GOLDEN-PLOVER
(*Pluvialis fulva*)

In breeding plumage, Pacific Golden-Plovers differ from American Golden-Plovers in that there is much white on the flanks and on the undertail coverts. In other plumages, the two species are nearly identical.

The migratory patterns of these two closely related species are, nonetheless, quite dissimilar. The two may, however, be seen together on the West Coast in fall. Pacific Golden-Plovers breed in Siberia and northwestern Alaska. They winter in southeast Asia, Australasia, and on tropical Pacific Islands. Alaskan breeders migrate over the Pacific Ocean and many winter in Hawaii. On the West Coast, migrants are very rare in spring and are seen only in small numbers in fall; a very few winter in California.

SNOWY PLOVER
(*Charadrius alexandrinus*)

The Snowy Plover is a small, dainty, sand-colored waif of a plover that disappears from sight as it stops and starts its way across the sandy beaches and alkali flats upon which it nests. It breeds on five continents; in Europe, it is known as Kentish Plover.

Nests are shallow hollows in the sand. The eggs are often destroyed by humans, by flooding, or by predators, but the birds almost always attempt to renest. When the first nest succeeds, females may double-brood, and even triple-brood, with new mates.

Snowy Plovers are white below and pale tan above—Gulf Coast birds are pale *gray* above—with partial breast bands, dark ear patches, and dark bars across the top of their crowns. The males are more strongly marked than females.

Snowy Plover

The legs of Snowy Plovers range from dark gray to silver gray. The black bills, long and slender for a plover, are used to pick a wide variety of insects and aquatic invertebrates from sand beaches, and both tidal and salt flats.

Juveniles have no dark markings about the head, face, or neck, and the legs are lighter-colored. Nonbreeding plumage is a darker tannish-brown above than breeding plumage. The breeding and non-breeding plumages are similarly patterned, but in non-breeding plumage the dark markings are dull brown, rather than black.

Most interior populations migrate to coastal areas, and some coastal populations move south along U.S. and Central American coasts. Recently, the U.S. Fish and Wildlife Service designated the Pacific Coast population as "Threatened."

Wilson's Plover

WILSON'S PLOVER
(*Charadrius wilsonia*)

Wilson's Plover can be separated from all other single-banded North American plovers on the basis of its long, heavy bill. The large, entirely black bill is used to capture its favorite prey items—fiddler and other small crabs. Also consumed are marine worms, small mollusks, shrimp, and a variety of aquatic insects.

Wilson's Plover, a shade darker on average than the Piping and Snowy Plovers, features a broad neck band that is black on the male and brown on the female. The breast band may or may not appear complete across the breast. The legs are dull flesh-colored.

Nonbreeding birds of both sexes resemble breeding females, as do the juveniles. Young birds, however, have their darker brown upperparts neatly fringed buff. As in other small plovers, the scaly or scalloped juvenile pattern is evident at close range.

The western race breeds coastally from central Baja California south to Peru. The eastern race, which nests on southern Atlantic, Gulf, Caribbean and northern South American coasts, is declining, especially in the northern part of its range. Atlantic birds winter in Florida. Most Gulf and Mexican breeders remain year-round. Some Wilson's Plovers migrate as far south as northeastern Brazil.

Semipalmated Plover in breeding plumage

SEMIPALMATED PLOVER
(*Charadrius semipalmatus*)

This small, dark, singled-banded plover is a common sight wherever migrant shorebirds gather on muddy flats. Their "step, step, stop" routines make them stand out as they feed among swirling masses of foraging Least and Semipalmated Sandpipers. ("Semipalmated" refers to the partial webbing between the front toes.)

Semipalmated Plovers breed on Far North tundra and taiga as far south as the shores of northwestern British Columbia, Hudson Bay, and Nova Scotia. There are several records of pairs breeding far to the south of their normal range. The eggs are laid in a shallow scrape on pebbly or gravelly ground.

The male in breeding plumage features a black breast band and face mask, and a thin, faint supercilium ("eyebrow"). The breast band and face mask are blackish-brown in the female, which has a small but distinct white supercilium. Adults have orange legs and short, stubby, black-tipped orange bills with which they capture a wide variety of small invertebrates. The juvenile has a dark bill and a distinct supercilium; the upperparts appear scalloped when good views are attained.

Nonbreeding plumage is similar to but duller than breeding plumage; the bill is entirely dark. Semi Plovers winter coastally from the southern United States to southern South America.

P I P I N G   P L O V E R
(*Charadrius melodus*)

Various populations of Piping Plovers are federally listed as Threatened and Endangered. Their fragile nesting areas are often destroyed by and intruded upon by humans.

Management practices on the breeding grounds—the fencing of nesting areas, the use of predator exclosures, access restrictions, and predator control—are working well in some areas where studies show that fledging rates have doubled. Conservation efforts on wintering grounds, however, have been virtually nonexistent.

The cryptic, disruptive patterning of these (and other) plovers camouflages them well; they blend with shells and shadows and seem to disappear. Piping Plovers are pale above, the color of dry sand.

In breeding plumage, they have black breast bands that may—especially in females—be incomplete. There is a black bar across the top of the crown reaching almost from eye to eye. The females are not as distinctly patterned as the males.

Piping Plover male

The forehead, neck, and underparts are pure white. The legs are orange. The short, stubby, orange bill with its black tip is used to capture tiny marine worms, insects, crustaceans, and mollusks from the surface of flats.

These plovers breed on open, sandy Atlantic beaches from southern Canada to North Carolina. Interior populations breed on alkali flats in the Northern Great Plains and on sand and gravel beaches along the shores of the western Great Lakes. The well-camouflaged eggs are laid in slight hollows that are occasionally lined with beach debris. All populations migrate to southern Atlantic and Gulf Coast beaches.

In nonbreeding and juvenal plumage, Piping Plovers lack the breast and crown markings. The bills are blackish. The feathers of the juvenile bird's upper-parts are fringed off-white and the legs are dull yellowish-orange. At any season their soft, clearly whistled *"peep-lo"* call is a delight to both the ear and the soul.

Killdeer in breeding plumage

KILLDEER
(*Charadrius vociferous*)

The Killdeer is surely the best known and most widespread of all North American shorebirds. It breeds everywhere on the continent but in the Far North.

It nests in grassy fields, farm fields, meadows, pastures, driveways, between railroad ties, on golf courses, stony beaches, subarctic tundra, and graveled and tarred roofs. The nest is a slight depression lined with pebbles, grasses, or weed stalks.

The Killdeer's double breast band, bright reddish-orange rump, and loud piercing *"dee, dee, dee"* call are distinctive. All three plumages are similar. The black bill, relatively long and thin, is perfectly suited for a bird with a 98 percent insect diet.

Seeing singles and pairs of this species is the norm, but larger groups often gather on migration. Many years ago, I watched a flock of fifty-three migrant Killdeer fly south above Jamaica Bay Wildlife Refuge on a cool September morning. Most retreat south in winter, but a few remain in southern Canada and the northern United States.

Mountain Plover

MOUNTAIN PLOVER
(*Charadrius montanus*)

The misnamed Mountain Plover is actually a bird of the high plains and arid regions of the West. It is one of only a few shorebirds that lives away from water.

Mountain Plovers breed on short-grass prairies primarily in Montana, Wyoming, and Colorado. The nests are little more than depressions in dry ground. They winter in the Southwest in a narrow band from the interior valleys of California to southern Texas and northern Mexico. Preferred habitats at this season include bare dirt, short-cut sod and alfalfa fields.

This bird is very plain—pale brown above and white below with a buffy wash on the sides of the breast and a whitish supercilium.
In breeding plumage, both sexes show dark lores (the space between the eyes and the base of the bill), a dark crown bar, and a white forehead.

Juveniles are darker brown above with buff-fringed feathers. They have a buffy supercilium and flecks of dark brown at the sides of the breast. All Mountain Plovers have slim black bills and large eyes that make capturing their insect prey a snap. The legs are pale or yellowish brown.

Though I've searched for this species in July at Pawnee National Grasslands, Colorado, and on farm fields in southern California in winter, the next one that I see will be my first.

A M E R I C A N   O Y S T E R C A T C H E R
(*Haematopus palliatus*)

This large, showy shorebird is common in coastal salt marshes and on sandy beaches. The eastern race breeds on Atlantic and Gulf Coasts from New England south to the Texas coast. The western race inhabits the shores of western Mexico and Central America.

In open, sandy areas, this species scrapes out its nest, which is simply a shallow depression lined with tiny pebbles and bits of shell and dried seaweed. In marshy spots, the nest is often lined with reeds.

The American Oystercatcher's bright red-orange bill is sturdy and laterally flattened like that of its close relative, the Black Oystercatcher. It is used to open mussels, and in the southern part of its range, oysters. Unlike their western cousins,

American Oystercatcher in breeding plumage

these birds often probe for sandworms and for soft-shell clams.

These birds have black heads and necks, dark blackish-brown upperparts, white wing and uppertail patches, white underparts, and dull flesh-colored legs. Juveniles are similarly patterned in brown and white, with the dark feathers of the upperparts sporting buff fringes. The young bird's bill is pinkish-brown, dusky black toward the tip.

Nonbreeding plumage is virtually identical to breeding plumage. In late fall, it is thought that only birds from mid- and northern Atlantic regions migrate south. On the Atlantic Coast, this species has successfully expanded its range northward; populations have increased dramatically over the past two decades.

BLACK OYSTERCATCHER
(*Haematopus bachmani*)

This large, black, strikingly handsome shorebird breeds and winters along rocky Pacific shores from the Aleutians to Baja California. Its large, sturdy, orange-red bill is laterally flattened, perfectly adapted for opening their preferred shellfish prey.

The nest bowl, found above the high-tide line, is a depression in sand or fine gravel lined with shell fragments and tiny pebbles. Adults feed in the intertidal zone and feed the young well after they are able to fly.

Adult Black Oystercatchers have dark blackish-brown plumage and black heads and necks. They appear all-black at a distance. The legs are light pink or flesh-colored. Birds in juvenal plumage exhibit buff fringes on the feathers of the upperparts. The juvenile's bill is dull orange, dusky brown toward the tip.

In fresh nonbreeding plumage the belly feathers are finely tipped white, but these feathers wear quickly to blackish brown. Many Black Oystercatchers migrate short distances after the breeding season is complete and join fairly large flocks in mussel-rich areas, but some singles and pairs remain in one area year-round.

BLACK-NECKED STILT
(*Himantopus mexicanus*)

Black-necked Stilts are tall, slim, gregarious waders. They breed, always around water, in a variety of habitats in the western United States, and locally (that is, in limited areas of specific habitat) in the Southeast. When a stilt stands on dry land, its long, pink or reddish-pink legs seem to go on forever.

They feed both in the water and ashore; their long, needle-like black bills are used to capture a great variety of both aquatic and terrestrial insects.

Males are glossy black above with contrasting white underparts. Females are brownish-black above. Juveniles have dark brown upperparts with the feathers fringed in buff. In all plumages the head, face, and back of the neck are dark. The dark hindneck extends as a hook-shaped mark onto the sides of the upper breast. The forehead and a spot over the eye are white.

Because of its flashy appearance, these birds must depend on aggressive behavior (rather than camouflage) to defend their nest sites and young. The nests, often in conjunction with the nests of other pairs of both stilts and avocets, are shallow depressions made either on islands or along the shores of lakes, ponds, or stagnant pools.

In winter they appear exactly as they do in breeding plumage. After the breeding season, they migrate to coastal areas in the southern United States, and Central and northern South America.

Black-necked Stilt

AMERICAN AVOCET
(*Recurvirostra americana*)

The American Avocet, far more common in the West than in the East, is an elegant, strikingly beautiful gray-blue-legged wader that prefers shallow lakes, sloughs, and marshes year-round. A variety of aquatic insects, crustaceans, tiny shrimp and fishes, and other invertebrates are captured as these birds swish their slim, upcurved bills through the water.

A variety of elaborate courtship rituals have been observed. At a small pond in Imperial Beach, California, I saw a crouched female stand with her neck out-stretched for more than a minute, her chin nearly touching the water. A male walked around her several times, preening occasionally. He jumped on her back, copulated quickly, then stood beside her and placed one wing over her back as they crossed bills.

American Avocets breed mainly on sun-baked flats near saline, usually alkaline, lakes on North American prairies, on lakes and marshes in the Great Basin, and at coastal estuaries and ponds on the West Coast. Three or four eggs are laid in a simple hollow lined with grasses. The nest is often rebuilt with sticks and feathers if it is threatened by rising waters.

Males and females are similarly feathered in all plumages. The female's bill, however, is shorter and more strongly upcurved than the male's. In breeding plumage, avocets are white and black above and white below, with rust-colored hoods that extend almost to the belly.

Avocets in fresh juvenal plumage are similar to adults, though clearly paler, with a cinnamon wash on the crown and the back of the neck. They are commonly seen in juvenal plumage *only* on the breeding grounds; feather wear and the onset of molt to first-winter plumage renders them virtually indistinguishable from adults during migration and on the wintering grounds.

In nonbreeding plumage a grayish hood replaces the rust-colored one. American Avocets are medium-range migrants; some fly as far as 2,000 miles to wintering grounds on southern U.S. and Mexican coasts.

American Avocet in breeding plumage

G R E A T E R   Y E L L O W L E G S
(*Tringa melanoleuca*)

Among the earliest northbound migrants, Greater Yellowlegs are tall, hand-some shorebirds; their long legs range from yellow to orange in color. While living in New York City, I knew that spring was on its way after spotting the first Greater Yellowlegs foraging in the shallows at Jamaica Bay Wildlife Refuge.

In all plumages, it is best separated from Lesser Yellowlegs by its larger size, its longer, heavier bill (which is often slightly upturned and lighter colored at the base), and by its louder, more strident call—a whistled string usually consisting of three or more emphatic *"tew, tew, tew"* notes. Lesser Yellowlegs are smaller and slimmer, and have dark, straight, thinner bills. Their call is a flatter *"tew"* or *"tew, tew."*

Greater Yellowlegs breed mainly on the sphagnum bogs that stretch across the continent from southern Alaska through the northern prairie provinces to Labrador and Newfoundland. The eggs are laid in a slight depression in muskeg mosses.

Greater Yellowlegs' breeding plumage is dark blackish-brown above with bold white spotting. Below, it is white with heavy spotting and streaking on the neck and breast, and bold bars and chevrons (V shapes) on the sides of the belly. The barring sometimes extends to the belly as well.

Greater Yellowlegs juvenile molting to first winter plumage (left) and adult molting to winter plumage

Adult birds in worn breeding plumage head south as early as mid-June. During southbound migration, freshly plumaged juveniles, with feathers neatly spotted and notched, are easily distinguished from the worn adults. Young birds routinely linger along northern U.S. coasts until November, and a few winter there. On migration, Greaters frequent freshwater and salt-marsh pools and flats, and a variety of other wetland habitats. They winter on all southern U.S. coasts and in Central and South America. In nonbreeding plumage, the feathers of the pale-gray upperparts are finely spotted, notched and fringed white.

Greater Yellowlegs feed on tiny fishes, aquatic insects, crabs, and other invertebrates by pecking them out of the water. At times, especially when feeding in groups, they rush forward through the water, plowing their bills straight ahead or swinging them from side-to-side, catching small prey items as they go.

The ever-wary Greater Yellowlegs earns its nicknames, "great tattler" and "greater tell-tale," from its habit of screaming alarm notes at the slightest provocation, often flushing and dispersing large mixed flocks of roosting shorebirds.

LESSER YELLOWLEGS
(*Tringa flavipes*)

Lesser Yellowlegs is a slim, dainty wader with a slim, straight bill. In all plumages, it is very similar to the Greater Yellowlegs. In breeding plumage, though, the streaks on the breast never extend onto the belly as they often do on Greaters. When the two species are side-by-side, Greaters are well larger than Lessers.

Lessers breed on bogs and marshes in the spruce forests of central Alaska and western and central Canada. The southern part of their breeding range overlaps that of Greater Yellowlegs, but Lessers tend to nest in drier areas. The nest is a simple depression atop a hillock or ridge, usually in a cleared or burned-over area.

Lessers feed on a variety of aquatic insects. They migrate later than Greaters

Lesser Yellowlegs juvenile

in spring and earlier in fall. The bulk of migration is south and east and then across the Atlantic to wintering grounds the length and breadth of South America. Some winter on southern U.S. and Central American coasts.

The ornithological literature states that Lessers are more apt to be seen in large flocks than Greaters. But for the eight years that I conducted International Shorebird Survey (ISS) counts at Jamaica Bay Wildlife Refuge, Lessers were always encountered in loosely associated feeding groups numbering from a handful to a few dozen, while Greaters regularly roosted in large flocks of from 100 to 500 or more birds.

SOLITARY SANDPIPER
(*Tringa solitaria*)

True to its name, the Solitary Sandpiper is usually seen alone. It is extremely rare to see a group of more than three or four. Solitaries bob up and down as they search deliberately for aquatic insects and small crustaceans along the edges of shallow freshwater pools or along the shores of woodland ponds or streams. The presence of a fly-over Solitary Sandpiper is often revealed by its shrill *"peet weet"* call.

This species is dark gray-brown above, lightly spotted white. It has greenish legs, a fairly short, straight bill, and a prominent, complete eye-ring. The throat, neck and breast are streaked dark brown. All plumages are similar, but in fresh juvenal plumage the spotting is brighter and more evident. Amazingly, this species nests in *trees* in the boreal forests of Canada and Alaska, frequently using the old nests of Rusty Blackbirds, robins, grackles, and waxwings. Solitary Sandpipers migrate south across a broad front, primarily east of the Rockies. A few winter in the southern United States, most in the Caribbean region and from Central America south to Argentina.

WILLET
(*Catoptrophorus semipalmatus*)

The Willet is a large, stocky, gray shorebird with blue-gray legs and a medium-long, straight bill. It's loud *"pill, will, willet"* call is uttered only on its breeding territory. At rest, it appears plain, but with its wings raised, it is transformed into a strikingly handsome creature; the broad white wing band is distinctive.

Breeding Willets are grayish-brown above barred blackish, and are heavily barred on the breast and the flanks. In nonbreeding plumage they are simply gray above and white below. The western race breeds on the Great Plains and in the Prairie Provinces and winters primarily on the Pacific Coast south of Washington; some winter on the Gulf Coast and southeastern U.S. coasts as well.

The eastern race breeds on Atlantic and Gulf Coasts. Northern breeders move south coastally, but some southern birds do not migrate at all. After most eastern birds have moved south, some western Willets make it to the East Coast. They are lighter gray and larger than the eastern birds.

Willets breed in a wide variety of habitats. The location and structure of their nests are also extremely variable. Coastal nests are often concealed in tall marsh grasses or under shrubs. Inland nests are found on prairies, in short marsh grass, or on alkali flats. Eggs may be laid in shallow or deep depressions or in well-constructed nests of grasses and weeds built on open sand. The feathers of the upperparts of juvenile Willets are neatly edged buff.

WANDERING TATTLER
(*Heteroscelus incanus*)

After breeding near Alaskan mountain streams, this species migrates to rocky wintering grounds along the Pacific Coast from central California to Ecuador, and to remote Pacific islands from Hawaii west to the northeastern coast of Australia. Nests may be simple hollows on gravel bars or well constructed of roots and twigs. Wandering Tattlers are uniformly gray above with dull yellow legs and a blackish bill. In breeding plumage they are grayish white below and heavily barred blackish. Nonbreeding and juvenile birds have a gray wash on the neck, breast, and flanks.

On breeding grounds, tattlers feed mostly on the larvae of aquatic insects; on the wintering grounds, they feed on mollusks. This bird usually nods its head and totters while feeding.

SPOTTED SANDPIPER
(*Actitis macularia*)

Spotted Sandpipers on migration are a common sight. They frequent virtually all wet habitats at both coastal and inland locations, teeter-tottering as they search for their prey—a wide variety of both aquatic and terrestrial insects. The latter are routinely snapped out of midair.

This widespread species breeds in all but southern and far northern North America in a variety of habitats, at times at altitudes as high as 14,000 feet. Nests may be sparsely lined hollows in the ground or deep cups of grasses or mosses. Females are, at times, polyandrous. Sex-role reversal is the rule for Spotteds— the females court the males and defend the territories, their mates tend the eggs and young.

Spotted Sandpipers in breeding plumage are brown above and heavily spotted below. In nonbreeding and juvenal plumages, the upper parts are grayish-brown, the underparts white. Juvenile birds feature wing covert feathers marked with wavy dark bars.

Spotteds migrate south in a wide front across the continent and winter in the southern United States (usually coastally), the Caribbean, and from Central America south to northern Argentina and Chile. They fly on stiff, rapidly beating wings with shallow wingbeats, except on prolonged flight during migration where they fly with deep wingbeats like other shorebirds.

Upland Sandpiper
(*Bartramia longicauda*)

This odd-looking brown shorebird almost never visits the shore, preferring instead a variety of grassy habitats: pastures, prairies, alfalfa fields, golf courses, and airports. It is a widespread and extremely local nester; its crescent-shaped range extends from southeastern Alaska to central prairies and Great Plains to the northeastern United States (where numbers are declining.)

Uppies are long-winged, small-headed, and large-eyed, with long, thin necks, and long, yellowish legs. The three plumages are similar: dark crown, dirty-grayish face, blackish-brown buff-fringed feathers above; neck, hindneck, and breast are buffy with dark streaks grading to dense chevrons and barring on the flanks. Juveniles have a scalier look and buffier faces.

They are often seen with just their head and neck showing above the grass, and at times on fenceposts. The liquid, rolling *"pulip, pulip"* call often brings attention to fly-overs. Migration to southern South American wintering grounds is mainly through the interior of both continents, but some use the East Coast in fall as well.

Whimbrel
(*Numenius phaeopus*)

The wild, rolling, whistled call of the Whimbrel seems to be born of the ocean waves over which it flies. Its strongly decurved bill and boldly striped crown help identify it. Whimbrels dine on a variety of shorebird fare (including berries on the breeding grounds). Their favorite winter foods include sand crabs on the Pacific Coast and fiddler crabs in Florida.

Whimbrels are always dark brown above, light below. The neck and breast are streaked brown and the feathers of the upperparts are spotted, edge-notched,

Upland Sandpiper in breeding plumage

and fringed whitish-buff. The juvenile upperpart feathers are more neatly spotted and edge-notched, giving them a crisply patterned look.

Whimbrels nest on grassy tundra hummocks. They migrate along both coasts and winter mainly from California south to Chile, and on south Atlantic, Gulf, Caribbean, and northern South American beaches. Nonbreeding plumage resembles breeding plumage though it is often a shade lighter.

LONG-BILLED CURLEW
(*Numenius americanus*)

This species is North America's largest sandpiper. It is named for its call, a musical *"cur-lee"* and for its long, decurved bill, that in females—the larger sex—may approach 9 inches in length!

In North America it can be confused with a Whimbrel, which is smaller and grayer and shows a prominently striped head. At rest, with its bill tucked in its scapulars, Long-billed Curlews can be indistinguishable from Marbled Godwits; the size difference is not always apparent.

Now primarily a western breeder, the Long-billed Curlew formerly nested on prairies east of the Mississippi River in areas now planted with corn and wheat. In the last century, migrants were slaughtered by market hunters. They still breed on prairies and grasslands from the west-central United States to the prairie

Long-billed Curlew

provinces. The eggs are laid in a grass-lined hollow. In breeding plumage this species is cinnamon-brown with black and buff speckling above, and cinnamon-buff below. It has bright cinnamon buff wing linings and grayish-blue legs. Nonbreeding and juvenal plumages are nearly identical to breeding plumage. This species is a medium-distance migrant, dispersing to the coasts of California, Central America, and the Gulf of Mexico.

The tip of the upper mandible is soft and is used to feel for prey items. On prairies these birds feed on grasshoppers, crickets, beetles, and earthworms. On migration and in winter they find similar prey in plowed fields, but they favor salt marshes, mud flats along rivers and estuaries, and sandy beaches where they capture fiddler crabs, other crustaceans, and small fishes and amphibians.

Hudsonian Godwit juvenile

HUDSONIAN GODWIT
(*Limosa haemastica*)

This tall, dark, handsome shorebird is one of my favorites. After flocking at James Bay, Canada, in fall, they are not seen again in substantial numbers until they reach southern South America. Some ornithologists believe that their flight over oceans and jungles between these two points is made *nonstop*!

The Hudsonian Godwit, a bit smaller than the Marbled, has three distinct plumages. In breeding dress, the males have dark brick-red breasts, bellies, and undertail coverts and are heavily barred on the flanks. The females are somewhat duller and larger than their mates. The bills of birds in breeding plumage are orange based with blackish tips.

The dark-centered feathers of the young bird's upperparts are neatly fringed rufous-buff, and the neck and breast are washed golden-buff. Nonbreeding birds are plain gray above and white below. In fall, when they are seen on the East Coast, molting birds will still show flecks of brick-red on their breasts. It is likely, though, that most fly over North America without stopping on their way to the wintering grounds in southern Argentina. Adults are seen in the interior on spring migration.

The legs are always dark blue-gray. The long, pointed, slightly upturned bills are ideal for probing for marine worms, crustaceans, mollusks, and insect larvae. In juvenal and nonbreeding plumages the bills are pink based (sometimes orange-pink) with blackish tips. In powerful flight, the Hudsonian Godwit's dark wing linings, narrow white wingstripes, and showy white rump are good identification characteristics.

MARBLED GODWIT
(*Limosa fedoa*)

The Marbled Godwit is named for the marbled pattern of its upperparts and for its *"ger-WHIT"* call. It is a western species that breeds in grassy meadows in the interior of northern North America. The nest is simply a hollow in the grass.

A medium-distance migrant, it is common in winter on the West Coast from Oregon to Central America, and less common, but regular, from Virginia to Florida and on the Gulf Coast.

In the mid-nineteenth century it was an abundant fall migrant on the Atlantic Coast from New England southward, but was decimated by market hunters; its numbers have increased there in the fall during the past decade, but it is still fairly rare north of Virginia.

Marbled Godwits are nearly identical to Long-billed Curlews in both color and pattern, but as long as the bills are visible, identification is easy. Marbleds are cinnamon-brown above speckled black and buff, and cinnamon buff below. The wing linings are bright cinnamon buff, the legs grayish-blue. Females average slightly in size, and are somewhat longer-billed than males.

Marbled Godwits have long, slightly upcurved, bi-colored bills. Birds in breeding plumage are heavily streaked and barred on the breast. At the height of breeding plumage, the base of the bill is brownish-orange. At all other times, the base of the bill is pink.

Marbled Godwits feed by probing deeply into wet sand, mud, or soil. Though their diet is similar to that of Long-billed Curlews, Marbled Godwits eat more grubs and other insect larvae and consume tubers and the seeds of some aquatic plants as well. On Pacific wintering beaches they feast regularly on sand crabs.

RUDDY TURNSTONE
(*Arenaria interpres*)

In late May, on the coarse-sand beaches along the Delaware Bay shore, it is not uncommon to see many thousands of Ruddy Turnstones along with equal numbers of Red Knots and Sanderlings, all feeding frantically on horseshoe crab eggs to fuel the last leg of their journey to their breeding grounds on the shores of the Arctic Ocean. It is the turnstones that lead the onslaught by digging up the horseshoe crab egg-nests.

The Ruddy Turnstones are in their distinctive black, white, and chestnut-red breeding colors at this time; their harlequin pattern is even more striking in flight. The males are brighter and more boldly marked about the face than the females.

Ruddy Turnstones breed on coastal plains and lowlands around the Arctic Ocean. The nest is just a depression in the tundra lined with dry plant matter. In nonbreeding plumage they are similarly patterned, but considerably duller: brown above, with a brownish rather than black bib. Juveniles look similar to adults in winter plumage except that the back feathers are neatly fringed whitish-buff, giving the young birds a scalloped appearance. The rest of the feathers of

Ruddy Turnstone male in breeding plumage

the upperparts are often fringed rufous.

In all plumages their short legs are orange, and their short, stout, pointed, slightly upturned bills are black or blackish-brown. On migration, Ruddy Turnstones prefer stony, rocky, and sandy coastal beaches. They winter on all U.S. coasts southward to Argentina and Chile.

Their diet is incredibly varied and includes sand fleas, marine worms, mollusks, decaying fish flesh, fly larvae and other insects. The soft parts of barnacles, fiddler crabs, tern eggs, berries, and even bread are regularly consumed. It is a treat to see one "turning stones" while feeding.

BLACK TURNSTONE
(*Arenaria melanocephala*)

For much of each year, Black Turnstones are a common sight along rocky Pacific coastlines. They take flight when a large wave threatens to swamp them, their stark black and white patterns cutting low above the water. They feed mainly on barnacles and limpets and are well camouflaged on the dark rocks.

The breeding plumage is quite handsome, nearly all jet-black above with a thin, white supercilium, and a large white spot behind the bill. Some white is visible on the folded wing. The jet-black bib is finely streaked white at the sides. The bill is dark and the legs reddish-black. They head north in April and May to breed on Alaskan coastal tundra.

By mid-July, adults are back on their rocky Pacific wintering grounds. In nonbreeding plumage the upperparts and bib are uniformly blackish-brown. Juveniles, which arrive in August, are nearly identical to the nonbreeding adults, but can be easily distinguished by their unworn feathers and neat appearance.

Black Turnstone in nonbreeding plumage

S U R F B I R D
(*Aphriza virgata*)

After breeding on mountain ridges in central Alaska and the Yukon Territory, Surfbirds winter almost exclusively on rocky Pacific coasts from southern Alaska south to Tierra del Fuego! North of Baja, they are usually seen in the company of Black Turnstones. After opening mussels, turnstones eat the soft parts; Surfbirds eat the whole mussel, then regurgitate the shells.

Surfbirds are chunky, medium-sized shorebirds with short, heavy legs, thick toes, thick necks, and short, plover-like bills. These adaptations make it easy for them to climb rocks and tear shellfish from their attachments.

The head and upperparts are gray, and the breast and upper belly heavily

Surfbird in nonbreeding plumage

streaked. In fresh breeding plumage the dark scapulars may be notched rusty-orange or have black or white tips. Worn adults are even darker above, the rusty-orange markings having faded. The legs are yellowish and the base of the bill is dull orange.

In the briefly held juvenal plumage, the upperparts are neatly fringed whitish; the back, head, neck and upper belly are gray with fine white speckling. Nonbreeding Surfbirds are similar to juveniles but are more solidly gray above with streaked flanks and a whitish chin.

RED KNOT
(*Calidris canutus*)

Four races of this stocky, short-necked shorebird breed locally on rocky or gravelly ground in high arctic regions worldwide. Their nest is a rocky hollow. North American birds breed near Point Barrow, Alaska, and on high arctic islands, including Banks, Baffin, Ellesmere, and Victoria.

Some North American populations winter on southern U.S. coasts, especially on Florida's west coast and on large tidal bays in California. Many migrate to southern South America, and still others routinely winter in western Europe by way of Iceland. Huge flocks of northbound South American birds stage in southeastern Brazil and then again on the Delaware Bay shore, where they feast on horseshoe crab eggs before heading for the Arctic.

Red Knots in breeding plumage are quite handsome with richly colored faces, necks, breasts and bellies ranging from orange-red to brick-red. Feathers of the upperparts are blackish gray edged in rufous or yellowish-buff and tipped silvery gray. The coverts are grayish and edged white. Worn, faded, southbound adults begin molting while on migration, and are often seen fully molted into the gray above/white below nonbreeding plumage by October.

Juveniles are neatly patterned; each gray feather of the upperparts has a thin black subterminal band and a whitish fringe. The typical scalloped juvenile look is evident. Juveniles have a prominent supercilium and are white below with fine gray streaks and spots on the neck and breast (which is washed buff in fresh juvenal plumage.) The legs are greenish and the bill is black in all plumages.

SANDERLING
(*Calidris alba*)

Though most sun worshipers have never heard the word "Sanderling," this small wind-up-toy sandpiper is surely the world's most familiar shorebird. On migration and in winter it is seen regularly on the beaches of six continents foraging in the wet sand left by retreating waves. Prey includes sand fleas, tiny mollusks and shrimp, and marine worms. Mysteriously, Sanderling populations have declined dramatically over the past few decades.

They breed locally on High Arctic tundra around the world, always near the Arctic Circle where they feed on flies, fly larvae, and other insects. Inexplicably, some fully molted birds in breeding plumage appear speckled gray, silver, black and white above and on the neck and breast, while in others the feathers of the upperparts are richly edged, fringed and tipped rust, rufous, or red-orange. In both cases the back and scapular feathers are blackish-centered, the coverts duller.

In North America, Sanderlings winter on virtually all U.S. and southern Canadian coasts south to the tip of southern South America. It is not known why some populations or age-classes remain far north while others migrate great distances. In nonbreeding plumage they are the whitest gray above of all wintering shorebirds. They sport pale gray caps and are pure white below.

Juvenile Sanderlings leave the Arctic in August, about a month after the adults. Fresh juveniles have a striking black and white checkerboard pattern on the upperparts, a streaked, dark-gray cap, and pure white underparts with fine streaking on the sides of the breast. At all times of year, this species shows a bright white wingbar in flight.

SEMIPALMATED SANDPIPER
(*Calidris pusilla*)

This small, very abundant shorebird migrates primarily up and down the Atlantic Coast on its way to and from northern and central South American coastal wintering areas. Central Canadian and Alaskan breeding populations travel through the interior of North America in spring. Semipalmateds breed on upland tundra near small lakes, ponds, and streams across the top of North America.

Except in the West, the Semipalmated Sandpiper is our most abundant peep. Semis are often confused with Leasts, but separating the two species can be easy. Leasts are generally browner, have slimmer, more pointed bills, and yellowish or light greenish legs.

Semis may also be confused with Westerns, which generally have longer, finer bills that are often drooped at the tip. Female Eastern Canadian Semis,

Semipalmated Sandpiper molting to nonbreeding plumage

though, will have bills longer than those of some male Westerns. (Male peeps are shorter-billed than females, and bill size increases in Semipalmated breeding populations from west to east.)

The Semipalmated Sandpiper has black legs, a short black bill with a blunt tip, and small webs (semipalmations) between the toes. In breeding plumage they are extremely varied. The crown is streaked. The upperparts have blackish- and brownish-centered feathers variably fringed gray and chestnut—some feathers have silver bases. The sides of the breast are variably streaked and spotted. Most birds appear gray overall, some more brownish. Above, fresh juveniles have dark-centered, neatly fringed feathers that give the bird a scalloped look. Individuals usually appear brownish overall, some appear grayish or blackish, while still others are more chestnut colored. In fresh juvenal plumage, all peeps have a buff wash on the breast.

Semipalmateds move forward constantly while foraging on wet mud, jabbing and picking aquatic invertebrate prey from the surface. Groups of juveniles are occasionally seen probing for prey items that are just below the surface. These birds hold their tails much higher in the air than they do when picking. A sea of quivering primary feathers gives the feeding flock an odd appearance.

WESTERN SANDPIPER
(*Calidris mauri*)

Considering its relatively small breeding range in western Alaska, it is surprising that this species is one of the Western Hemisphere's most common shorebirds. It is estimated that 6,500,000 visit the Copper River Delta in Alaska each spring, with one day counts of two million birds!

Huge migrant flocks gather at other Pacific staging areas. Substantial numbers migrate through the interior West and they are common on the East Coast in fall as well, with greater numbers occurring southward. On migration they favor coastal mud flats, and muddy margins of inland lakes and ponds.

The Western Sandpiper is the longest-billed of the peeps. Its tapered black bill has a pointed, drooped tip. Females are longer-billed than males, and slightly larger as well. In breeding plumage they have much chestnut-red in the scapulars, the ear coverts, and on the crown; they are whitish below with blackish spots on the breast and bold black chevrons on the flanks.

Juveniles are feathered similarly to Semipalmated Sandpipers, but a young Western's black-centered scapulars have bright rufous fringes. The coverts are gray-brown and neatly fringed whitish-buff. The scapulars and coverts, therefore, show much contrast; on young Semipalmateds there is little or no contrast between these two feather tracts. Young Westerns arrive on the West Coast

Western Sandpiper in breeding plumage

beginning in late July and about two weeks later in the East.

Western Sandpipers in non-breeding plumage are gray above and white below; the crown is gray and the neck and sides of the breast are finely streaked gray. Westerns winter coastally from the Pacific Northwest and the mid-Atlantic states south to northern South America.

L E A S T   S A N D P I P E R
(*Calidris minutilla*)

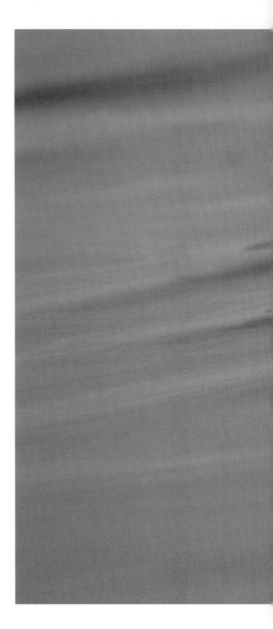

This small, fairly common peep is well named, as it is the world's smallest shorebird. Leasts nest in grass- or leaf-lined cups on subarctic tundra and in northern boreal forests, Alaska to Newfoundland.

This species migrates on a broad front across the continent, rarely forming large flocks like many of its counterparts. On migration, it is routinely seen inland on the grassy edges of lakes, ponds, and reservoirs. They feed on tiny prey that include sand fleas and other crustaceans, flies, and aquatic insects and their larvae.

In general, Leasts are browner than the Semis and Westerns. They have short, dark, slightly drooped bills with very fine tips. The legs range from greenish-yellow to yellow. In breeding plumage they have a streaked cap and an indistinct whitish supercilium; the feathers of the various upperparts are fringed yellow-buff, white, gray and rufous, but the bird has an overall brown look. In July and August when the fringes are totally worn, adults appear very dark brown.

The fresh juvenile is a gem-of-a-bird with the dark-centered back, scapular,

Least Sandpiper in nonbreeding plumage

and tertial feathers neatly fringed or edged bright orange-rufous, and the coverts fringed buff. Most scapulars are broadly tipped white, forming a white V when the bird is viewed from above.

Birds in nonbreeding plumage are gray above and white below; fresh feathers on the upperparts have dark shafts. They winter from the southern United States south through the northern half of South America.

121

White-rumped Sandpiper molting to nonbreeding plumage

WHITE-RUMPED SANDPIPER
(*Calidris fusicollis*)

This peep breeds on wet tundra along the far northern coasts. In fall, it flies southeast to the North Atlantic coast and then sets out over the Atlantic bound for northeastern coastal South America; they winter in southern South America. Generally a late spring migrant, it heads north largely through the interior.

Breeding plumaged White-rumpeds have streaked rusty crowns and rusty ear coverts. Most of the black-centered back and scapular feathers are fringed rufous, but some are broadly edged gray. The coverts have brownish centers with whitish fringes. In flight or with wings raised, the white rump is easily seen.

The breast is heavily spotted and streaked and the flanks have long, thin black streaks or small chevrons that are characteristic of the species. The bill is dark; the base of the lower mandible is orangeish. Worn, molting southbound adults are grayish overall and at a distance, appear gray-hooded.

White-rumped Sandpipers are distinctly larger and longer-winged than Semis and Westerns, on which the wings and tail are the same length; whereas a White-rumped's wings extend well beyond its tail. The remarkably long wings, together with its horizontal feeding posture, gives this species an elongated look (that is shared by Baird's Sandpiper).

White-rumpeds in juvenal plumage have brown-centered back and scapular feathers fringed rufous, and brownish-centered coverts fringed buff. Some lack the extensive rufous fringing and are much duller. The gray above/white below nonbreeding plumage is not attained until the birds reach South America.

Baird's Sandpiper juvenile

BAIRD'S SANDPIPER
(*Calidris bairdii*)

Baird's Sandpiper is structurally similar to White-rumped, but is slightly longer-winged, the wingtips often crossing. Its breeding range is also similar, but it extends farther north onto Arctic islands and farther west into Alaska.

In spring and fall, migration is through the center of the continent, but juveniles reach both coasts in fall. Baird's Sandpipers winter in western South America and Argentina. Migrant birds of this species prefer drier habitats to wet mud.

Baird's Sandpipers in breeding plumage have coarsely mottled upperparts with most feathers blackish-centered with buff fringes; but some are silver-gray based, and others still have silver-gray edges. The breast is brownish and finely streaked; the legs and bill are black.

Finding my first juvenile Baird's in New York City took six years of serious September searching, but when I finally found one, its extremely long wings, buffy face and breast, and scalloped look were all dead give-aways to its identity.

PECTORAL SANDPIPER
(*Calidris melanotos*)

This medium-sized sandpiper most closely resembles a large Least Sandpiper, but the breast streaking on this species is more prominent and contrasts more sharply with the white belly.

When breeding on coastal arctic tundra (in North America and Siberia), Pectorals have brown crowns and are brown above, neatly fringed buff. Males are larger, their breast markings blacker, and the breast sac—used to produce eerie hooting calls—is evident even when the bird is at rest.

In fall, Pectorals primarily migrate south and east, then south over the western

Pectoral Sandpiper in fresh juvenal plumage

Atlantic to South America. Most winter in southern South America. Nonbreeding plumage, not attained until birds reach the wintering grounds, resembles breeding plumage, but is lighter brown and duller.

Juveniles are similar to breeding adults, but are brighter, with black-centered upperparts fringed rufous or bright buff and usually with thin white stripes on the scapulars. On migration, they prefer the grassy margins of both inland and coastal ponds and wetlands where they forage for both terrestrial and aquatic insects.

P U R P L E   S A N D P I P E R
(*Calidris maritima*)

Visit any wave-tossed, mussel-covered jetty along New England or mid-Atlantic coasts in winter or early spring and you'll most likely find groups of Purple Sandpipers. In nonbreeding plumage, they are dark slate-gray (at times with a purple sheen) on the head, neck, breast, and upperparts and white below with dark gray streaks on the upper belly and flanks. The legs and the basal third of the bill are yellowish-orange.

Wintering birds can usually be found in good numbers well into May, when the last (largely unmolted) birds depart for breeding grounds in eastern Arctic Canada. (This species also breeds in Greenland, Iceland, and northern Europe— these birds winter in Scandinavia and western Europe.)

In breeding plumage, the Purple Sandpiper has a brown crown, brown upperparts variously fringed chestnut and white, a light supercilium, and reddish-brown ear coverts. The nape, chin, breast and flanks are finely streaked brown.

These hardy birds clamber surefootedly over slippery rocks even in freezing weather picking mussels, crabs, and small crustaceans as they go. On the breeding grounds their diet includes insects and insect larvae, small mollusks, algae, grasses, and mosses.

Purple Sandpiper

Rock Sandpiper in breeding plumage

ROCK SANDPIPER
(*Calidris ptilocnemis*)

The Rock Sandpiper, an uncommon western shorebird, is very closely related to the Purple Sandpiper. On their respective coasts, both inhabit rocky areas on migration and in winter.

A breeding-plumaged Rock Sandpiper resembles a large, stocky, short-winged Dunlin with a medium-sized black bill (somewhat decurved) and olive legs. The blackish patch is on the lower breast, not on the belly like a Dunlin's. The upperparts vary from fringed bright rufous to rather plain. They breed on upland tundra in extreme eastern Asia, on Bering Sea islands, and in western Alaska.

In nonbreeding and juvenile plumage Rock Sandpipers are virtually indistinguishable from the Purple Sandpiper. Rock Sandpipers winter regularly on jetties and rock outcroppings from southern Alaska south to northern California.

Dunlin in breeding plumage

DUNLIN
(*Calidris alpina*)

Dunlins are very abundant small sandpipers, a step up in size from the peep sandpipers. There are six recognized races worldwide that show considerable variation in size and in bill length.

The two American races, *pacifica* and *hudsonia*, are the largest and longest billed. The classic Dunlin has black legs, a fairly long decurved bill, and a short neck that results in a hunched look. Females on average are larger-sized and longer-billed than males.

In breeding plumage, the derivation of its former name, Red-backed Sandpiper, is evident; the back and the scapulars are edged rich chestnut-red. The wing-coverts are gray. A streaked neck and a black belly patch put the finishing touches on their spring dress.

Nonbreeding plumage is plain gray or grayish brown above, and white below with a grayish-brown wash across the breast. They strongly resemble winter plumaged Western Sandpipers, but are larger. (On winter Westerns, the wash is paler and confined to the sides of the breast, and is sometimes overlain with fine, blackish streaks.)

Juvenile Dunlins exhibit feathers of the upperparts neatly fringed buff and reddish-orange, but, unlike nearly all other shorebird species, the young begin the molt to first winter plumage *before* leaving the breeding grounds. When they arrive in the United States, gray winter feathers have replaced many of the fringed juvenile scapulars. In first-winter plumage, a few anterior scapulars, fringed reddish-orange, are retained at least through early fall. Dunlins are circumpolar breeders that utilize a variety of Arctic and sub-Arctic habitats. North American birds winter primarily along U.S. coasts, often well to the north of most other shorebirds, and often in great numbers.

On migration they feed on mud flats, probing for marine worms, sandfleas and other crustaceans, mollusks, and insects. Huge flocks are often seen in synchronous flight, twisting and turning and flashing light and dark as if a single creature.

CURLEW SANDPIPER
(*Calidris ferruginea*)

The Curlew Sandpiper is a medium-sized sandpiper with a slim black bill that is evenly decurved for its entire length. It nests on tundra in northern Russia, migrates in part through western Europe, and winters in Africa, southern Asia, and Australasia.

It wanders widely on migration, and adults are seen regularly on the Atlantic coast during both spring and early fall. This species has bred in Alaska, and increasing numbers of interior and West Coast records *may* be representatives of this population.

In fresh breeding plumage the Curlew Sandpiper is chestnut-red below; the individual feathers are fringed white. The black feathers of the upperparts are tipped

Curlew Sandpiper in breeding plumage

chestnut-red, silver, and white. All the light feather tips and edges wear quickly giving the bird a darker, overall look. Worn southbound adults (July to mid-October) usually show much chestnut-red below.

In nonbreeding plumage—basically brownish-gray above and white below—this species is paler-breasted than the very similar Dunlin (with which it associates regularly). Structurally, the Curlew Sandpiper is longer-winged and longer-legged than the Dunlin. Fresh juvenile Curlew Sandpipers are elegantly handsome with neat, pale-fringed upperparts and a golden-buff wash on the breast.

STILT SANDPIPER
(*Calidris himantopus*)

Stilt Sandpipers are often confused with Lesser Yellowlegs, but to me, they seem more like small, slim dowitchers. They commonly associate with dowitchers, and their sewing-machine-like feeding styles are similar as well. Stilts are easily separated from Lesser Yellowlegs; Stilts have a bolder whitish supercilium, greenish, not yellow legs, and their bills are drooped at the tip, not straight.

In breeding plumage Stilt Sandpipers are dark brown above, whitish below, and heavily barred dark brown on the breast and belly. The neck is streaked. The head features a dark crown, a prominent white supercilium and rich chestnut-red ear coverts. Worn, molting southbound adults are grayer brown with some barring below still evident, but with little color in the face.

In nonbreeding plumage they are similarly patterned but plain brownish-gray above. Fresh juvenile scapulars and coverts are neatly fringed buff; the back feathers are edged rufous. The breast is washed bronze. Young birds of this species begin to molt to first winter plumage on southbound migration; they exhibit gray backs and whitish-fringed wing coverts.

Stilt Sandpipers breed on tundra north of the tree-line. The bird's breast is rotated into the soft earth—usually atop a hummock—to form the inch-deep scrape nest. Migration in both spring and fall is largely through the interior; many use the Atlantic Coast as well. Stilt Sandpipers prefer inland wetlands and coastal pools. They winter primarily in central South America.

BUFF-BREASTED SANDPIPER
(*Tryngites subruficollis*)

The Buff-breasted Sandpiper is a medium-sized, elegantly handsome shorebird that breeds on the drier tundra of the north Alaskan coast and High Arctic islands. They move south across a broad front through the center of both Americas to wintering grounds on heavily-grazed South American pampas. Northbound migration is similar but routes are more restricted than in fall. All plumages are similar. Buff-breasteds have streaked brown crowns, buffy faces and breasts, and dark-centered feathers on the upperparts with buff or whitish fringes. The short bill is black, the medium-length legs yellow-ochre. Juveniles appear more scalloped above and are paler below, especially about the belly.

On migration, this species favors short-grass habitats and drying rice fields where it feeds primarily on fly and beetle larvae, other insects, and spiders; they rarely partake of marine invertebrates. Juveniles do frequent coastal ponds in fall, but are almost always seen on grassy margins.

Ruffs in breeding plumage, battling

RUFF
(*Philomachus pugnax*)

On migration, this Eurasian species wanders rarely but regularly to North America. Ruffs breed in northern Europe and Siberia and winter mainly in Africa. Some ornithologists believe that a few breed in Alaska. Like the Buff-breasted Sandpiper, this species employs a lek mating system, but the dancing arena and the male's individual territories are much smaller.

Prior to the breeding season, males of this species grow flamboyant frills of long feathers on the head and neck. The face is bare. No two of these extravagant feather "ruffs" are identical. Colors include white, gold, black, iridescent purple, brown and buff, at times in combination. The frills may be barred, speckled, or multi-colored. These amazing head tufts and neck plumes are used in a variety of courtship displays.

The smaller females (called reeves) and males in nonbreeding plumage are variably feathered grayish-brown or blackish above with white fringes. (Breeding females may show blackish blotches on the breast and flanks.) Juveniles are similar, but the face, neck, and breast are washed bright buff and the upperparts are neatly fringed buff. The leg and bill colors are seasonally variable. The short, slightly decurved bill is used to pick or probe for aquatic insects, worms, crustaceans, mollusks, algae, and weed seeds.

Short-billed Dowitcher worn juvenile

SHORT-BILLED DOWITCHER
(*Limnodromus griseus*)

Short-billed Dowitcher is a medium-sized, long-billed shorebird. Its bill is "short" only in comparison with those of most *female* Long-billed Dowitchers, and even in these instances there is some overlap. Three races of Short-billeds breed in open boggy areas in the boreal forests of North America: *caurinus* in the West, *hendersoni*, in central Canada, and *griseus* in eastern Canada.

Dowitchers feed by probing into soft mud with their long bills in sewing-machine-like fashion. Their diets include traditional shorebird fare. Both have grayish- to yellowish-green legs. In flight, both species show long, narrow white triangles on their lower backs.

In breeding plumage the breast and upper belly of the eastern and western races are salmon-orange to orange-red. The lower belly and undertail coverts are whitish. The sides of the upper breast are *spotted* and the flanks are barred. *Hendersoni* in breeding plumage is always salmon-orange *through to the undertail coverts* and the sides of the breast are only lightly spotted. The flanks are lightly barred.

In the gray above/white below nonbreeding plumage, and in juvenal plumage, which features orange-buff-fringed upperparts and buff-washed breasts, the races are virtually indistinguishable in the field. Separating breeding *caurinus* and breeding *griseus* is extremely difficult.

Short-billed Dowitchers migrate south across a broad front and winter coastally from the southern United States to northern South American coasts. Both adults and juveniles head south much earlier than adult and juvenile Long-billeds respectively. Away from their breeding areas, short-billeds prefer salt and brackish mud flats.

LONG-BILLED DOWITCHER
(*Limnodromus scolopaceus*)

The best way to separate Long-billed and Short-billed Dowitchers is by call. The Long-billed's sharp *"keek"* call is diagnostic. The Short-billed's call is a mellow *"tu tu tu"* or *"tu tuh lu."* The Long-billed's *"keek"* issued singly, is used as a contact call by feeding flock-mates; in rapid series, it serves as an alarm call when they take flight. Short-billeds call only when alarmed or (infrequently) in flight; feeding flocks are normally silent.

In breeding plumage, Long-billed Dowitchers are deep orange-red to brick-red below and are colored through to the undertail coverts. The sides of the upper breast as well as the flanks are usually densely barred.

Separating juveniles of these two species is easy. Juvenile Long-billeds, being grayer about the face, neck and upper breast, appear darker overall than juvenile Short-billeds. The tertial feathers of Long-billeds are plain gray with narrow rufous fringes that wear to grayish-white. The tertials of Short-billeds have orange internal markings, like irregular tiger stripes, and the young birds are much brighter overall than juvenile Long-billeds.

Understanding the timing of migration makes identification even simpler. Southbound juvenile Short-billeds migrate 5 to 8 weeks *before* juvenile Long-billeds. On the East Coast: A migrant dowitcher in fresh juvenile plumage in mid-August can only be a Short-billed; a dowitcher in fresh juvenal plumage in late September can only be a Long-billed, as juvenile Short-billeds will be worn and shabby looking by that time. (On the West Coast, migration dates are 2 to 3 weeks earlier.)

Long-billed Dowitchers breed on arctic tundra in northern and western Alaska and eastern Siberia. There is an easterly element to southbound migration; many are seen on the mid-Atlantic coast in fall. They are commonly seen in the western United States at this time. They winter on all southern U.S. coasts (a few inland) and throughout Mexico.

COMMON SNIPE
(*Gallinago gallinago*)

This secretive shorebird is rarely seen in the company of other shorebirds. In fact, it is rarely seen on the ground. When flushed, it explodes in zigzag flight uttering it's harsh, nasal alarm call, *"skaaap."* Prey is captured with its long bill which has an extremely sensitive, pliable tip. Food is mainly the larvae of aquatic insects, earthworms, crustaceans, mollusks, and even small salamanders and toads.

Snipes are bulky shorebirds with relatively short legs, long bills, boldly striped heads, and rusty reddish tails. The upperparts are blackish-brown variously streaked and barred buff. Broad buff strips run above the scapulars. All three plumages are virtually identical.

Common Snipes are widespread breeders in grassy meadows, bogs, and swamps from subarctic North American regions south to the central United States. They produce weird noises—"whoo, whoo, whoo, whoo"—during display flights by spreading their tail feathers during speedy dives.

Though some regularly remain in southern parts of breeding range, most winter in the southern United States, Mexico, Central America, and northern South America. Many move north in spring as early as February. Away from the breeding grounds this species prefers marsh edges and muddy ditches and farm ponds—the muddier the better.

Common Snipe

American Woodcock

AMERICAN WOODCOCK
(*Scolopax minor*)

The American Woodcock is similar to—and perhaps even stranger than—the Common Snipe. Both are still legally hunted in North America. Other similarities with the Snipe include bill length and sensitivity, secretive behavior, explosive flight when flushed, and early spring migration. (This species begins moving north in January.)

Its dumpy shape, short thick neck, rounded wings, nocturnal behavior, large high-set eyes, dark crown with three buff bars, and choice of nesting habitat—open woods and young forests—add to its "weirdness." Complexly patterned upperparts of dark brown, chestnut, and gray, along with gray-tipped orange-buff coverts and light orange-buff underparts make for perfect dead-leaf camouflage.

Woodcocks breed in extreme southeastern Canada and in the eastern United States. Above "singing fields" (open areas near breeding territories) males perform intricate display flights in early spring. The nests, leaf-lined depressions, are generally located in nearby woods. On warm winter and early spring nights, its *"peent"* call can be heard at dusk. Most winter in the southern portion of its range, but some remain north. Many often starve when long cold spells and snows freeze the ground and prevent them from feeding.

Wilson's Phalarope female in breeding plumage

WILSON'S PHALAROPE
(*Phalaropus tricolor*)

This small, swimming sandpiper is the largest and most terrestrial of the three phalaropes. It has the longest, slimmest bill. The toes feature lateral membranes, but are not truly lobed as in Red and Red-necked Phalaropes. It differs as well by wintering at fresh and brackish wetlands in southern South America; the other two phalarope species winter at sea.

With the sex roles reversed, female phalaropes are brightly colored, the males duller. The upperparts of females in breeding plumage are patterned pearly gray, rufous-red, and black. The crown, nape and hindneck are pearly gray. A black eye-mask continues down the neck and onto the back. The black blends with rufous-red which extends onto the sides of the breast.

The males are similarly patterned but much duller. Nonbreeding birds are gray above and white on the face and below, with a gray crown and a gray streak behind the eye. Juveniles are strikingly handsome with the dark brown feathers of the upperparts fringed reddish buff, and a golden buffish cast about the breast. Juvenal plumage is worn for only several weeks; most southbound migrant first-year birds are well molted into first winter plumage and show gray backs and scapulars that contrast with the juvenile coverts and tertials.

Wilson's are often absolutely frenetic as they forage while walking, wading, swimming, or spinning about on the water's surface. The diet is of aquatic insects and their larvae, brine shrimp, brine flies, and the seeds of some aquatic plants.

This species breeds primarily on the grassy shores of western and prairie wetlands, but has recently been expanding eastward. Nests are well concealed grass-lined hollows. This species begins moving south in early summer before any other North American shorebird.

RED-NECKED PHALAROPE
(*Phalaropus lobatus*)

The first Red-necked Phalarope in breeding plumage that I ever saw was one roosting on a sand spit in New York City with a large group of northbound migrant shorebirds; she stood out like a tiny jewel. In Churchill, dozens swam in the Granary Ponds, often pursuing and fighting over the duller males.

These birds are well named; the breeding female has a large bright chestnut red patch on the side of the neck that extends onto—and on some birds almost encircles—the upper breast. The neck is white, the crown and face nearly black, and there is a white mark above and just forward of the eye. The breast-band and upper flanks are dark ash-gray. The upperparts are black with two irregular yellow-buff stripes on each side.

The similarly (but indistinctly) patterned males are duller than the females with brown feathering replacing the black. Juveniles are dark above with extensive orange-buff edges and fringes. The thin, black, medium-sized bill is well-adapted for capturing all manner of minuscule aquatic invertebrates. The short legs and lobed toes help make them expert swimmers.

This species nests in grass-lined hollows worldwide on tundra near water. North American populations migrate at sea and along the West Coast in fall. They winter in the Pacific Ocean off Peru. Tens, even hundreds, of thousands formerly gathered in the mouth of the Bay of Fundy in early August, but numbers, in recent years have plummeted drastically.

Red-necked Phalarope female in breeding plumage

R E D   P H A L A R O P E
(*Phalaropus fulicarias*)

The Red Phalarope (Grey Phalarope in Europe) is the most pelagic (ocean-going) of its kind. With luck, small groups of storm-driven birds may be found at coastal locations, but most observers will need to take offshore boat trips to add this bird to their life lists.

This circumpolar breeder nests on high-arctic tundra, never far from the sea, in a well-concealed nest of domed grasses. The Red Phalarope has a shorter, thicker bill than the other phalaropes; it is yellow and black-tipped on breeding females, duller on males, and dark on juveniles.

Breeding females have dark brown crowns and forecrowns that encircle the base of the bill and extend to the chin. A large, bright white oval surrounds the eye. They are dark red-orange below and dark blackish-brown above with extensive bright buff edgings. Breeding males are similarly patterned but duller with streaked crowns.

Nonbreeding birds are white below and gray above with a black smudge through and behind the eye. The fore-crown is white and the black of the rear crown extends down the hindneck. Juveniles of this species have black upperparts broadly fringed orange-buff. The hindneck and back show blackish streaks of orange buff. The belly is white, the breast pinkish-buff. This species begins molting into first-winter plumage soon after fledging. As a result, young birds seen in the United States in August through November show partial or completely gray backs.

Reds winter at sea, primarily off Africa and western South America. Some winter offshore of California or Mexico. Like other phalaropes, they often feed by spinning in circles. With their larger bills, prey items average larger than those taken by other phalaropes. The diet includes small fish, jellyfish, beetles, flies, and crustaceans.

SHOREBIRDING

Chapter

9

horebirding can be as simple as walking along the beach in a bathing suit without any equipment at all. Watching Sanderlings race along the shoreline to and fro like so many wind-up toys or marveling at a thousand Dunlins wheeling above the waves in perfect unison can be exhilarating experiences even without the benefit of binoculars, spotting scope, or field guide.

All serious shorebird devotees, however, rely on a pair of quality binoculars, and most also include a tripod-mounted spotting scope in

their optical arsenals.

In many instances, because of access restrictions, ethical considerations, intervening stretches of soft mud, muck, or deep water (or an observer's desire to keep their feet dry), distant views of shorebirds are the best to be had. A quality pair of binoculars is, therefore, a necessity.

Although 7-power (7X) glasses are fine for general birding, 10-power binoculars are often preferred for shorebirding because the subjects are generally small and the viewing distances often great. Shorebirders who have difficulty holding 10X binoculars steady may prefer lighter 8-power glasses.

Birding magazines regularly publish reviews of both the classic models and the latest models. Before you plunk down your money, read as much material as you can, talk to other birders, and look through their binoculars. Then, buy the best glasses that you can afford. You will be rewarded by a lifetime of pleasurable (and usually maintenance-free) viewing.

Spotting scopes are terrestrial telescopes that offer magnification in the 15X to 60X range. The eyepieces for most models usually need to be purchased separately. Some observers prefer 15X, 20X, or 25X eyepieces. Others choose one of the above and add a 40-power eyepiece as well.

Because changing eyepieces in the field may cause problems, zoom eyepieces are often the choice of many shorebirders. For most scopes 15-40X and

American Avocet, nest distraction display

15-60X zooms are available. In all but the most expensive models the views provided in the 50-60X range are too dark for practical viewing.

Most major optical equipment manufacturers offer several spotting scope models, so do lots of research before investing in a spotting scope. And, as with binoculars, reviews of these products appear often in various birding periodicals. If a flimsy tripod is used, viewing will be difficult even with the finest spotting scope, especially in windy conditions—so be sure to do research in this area also.

Clothing requirements for shorebirding are minimal. In most cases, jeans that can stand a bit of mud or saltwater are fine. A long-sleeved shirt and a wide-brimmed hat will provide some protection from the sun. In colder weather, dress—of course—in layers.

Choosing suitable footwear is often a problem. Mid-calf rubber boots keep your feet dry, but may be uncomfortable on long walks and are often much too hot in summer when shorebirding is often excellent. In hot weather I prefer to wear an old pair of sneakers and get my feet wet, especially if I have access to a garden hose afterward!

Adding a few accessories before venturing afield can make shorebirding both safer and more pleasant. Sunscreen for the face and lips should be carried and applied liberally.

A belted or fanny-packed canteen can provide a much-needed cool drink during steaming hot weather. Lunch, your field notebook or notepad, insect repellent, and a field guide can be carried comfortably in a lightweight backpack. Excess layered clothing can be stored there as well. (Some observers—depending on how much they like to carry—prefer a birder's or lightweight photographer's vest.) Bring a soft pencil for sketching and a marking pen for writing field notes and you're ready to hit the beaches and mud flats.

In your field notebook, keep a record of all your shorebirding trips. Make note of the location, the date, the time and length of the trip, the weather, and the tidal stage or water level. Record the number of each shorebird species seen: Red Knot—38, Black-bellied Plover—17.

Be sure to keep a separate tally for each different habitat that you visit: East Pond mud flats (brackish): Least Sandpiper—43, Semipalmated Plover—9,

Baird's Sandpiper—1. Big John's Pond (freshwater): Spotted Sandpiper—2, Solitary Sandpiper—1.

Use common sense while shorebirding. Take care when traversing slippery mud flats and when clambering over rocks. And *always* respect "DANGER/SOFT MUD" signs. When I first began visiting the East Pond at the Jamaica Bay Wildlife Refuge I ignored one such sign and wound up waist-deep in the mud. I had to crawl out on my belly spread-eagle through the muck.

CONSERVATION

Chapter

10

I magine yourself a Red Knot, an exhausted, hungry Red Knot. You have just completed an eleven-day flight from Lagoa do Peixe, a lagoon in southern Brazil, to the shores of Delaware Bay, in Cape May County, New Jersey. When you left Brazil, after feasting on small snails, you weighed almost half a pound. Having converted the fat on your breast into the energy that fueled the 5,000 mile flight, you now weigh only half of that amount.

Bound for your breeding grounds on the Canadian high arctic, you must stop at the Delaware Bay shore—as Red Knots have been stopping for tens of thousands of years—to gorge yourself on horseshoe crab eggs and refuel for the last leg of your journey. Shorebird biologists have calculated that you will eat one of the tiny greenish eggs every five seconds, fourteen hours a day, for the next fourteen days. Though each egg is no bigger than a pencil point, the 90,000 or so knots that assemble here each spring consume about forty-four tons of them.

Your flock is confronted with a strange sight as it drops out of the sky expecting dinner. Instead of a white sand beach littered with tens of thousands of horseshoe crabs, a twenty-five mile strip of glistening black goo lies before you. Last night as you flew past the Outer Banks at an altitude of 17,000 feet, a tanker ran aground in Delaware Bay spilling 800,000 gallons of heavy industrial oil. You—and the entire New World populations of several common migrant shorebirds—are in peril.

T H E   B A D   N E W S

Recent analyses of shorebird population trends for 27 common eastern North American migrant species showed declines for 14 species. International Shorebird Survey (ISS) data indicated 40 to 80 percent declines in the number of Semipalmated Sandpipers, Short-billed Dowitchers, Sanderlings, and Whimbrels between 1974 and 1983—those declines continue today. Recent Canadian Wildlife Service studies revealed negative trends in 10 of 13 nesting shorebird species.

A shorebird's worst enemy is man. In the late 1800s they were shot by the wagonload for market; populations of several species were decimated. After more than half a century of protection, many have increased their numbers substantially. The Eskimo Curlew never recovered; it is, at very best, within a hair's breadth of extinction.

Today's shorebirds are rarely hunted for the market anywhere in South America, but subsistence hunting in one or two impoverished countries continues. Presently in the United States, only two species of shorebirds may be hunted legally: the Common Snipe and the American Woodcock.

As the twentieth century draws to a close, buckshot does far less damage than bulldozers. Visit a coastal area anywhere in the United States. What do you see? Residential communities, airports, extensive seaside resorts, golf courses, landfills, industrial parks, and huge marinas; mile after mile of wood, concrete, and steel. There just are not many marshes or mud flats left.

Fifty percent of the wetlands present in the United States 300 years ago have been destroyed. Of the approximately 90 million acres of remaining wetlands, less than 5 percent are salt or brackish. It is not surprising to learn that many species of shorebirds concentrate to an amazingly high degree at a relatively few locations along their migratory routes.

During fall migration in the decade of the 1980s, more than 60 percent of all shorebirds counted by ISS volunteers were at just ten staging areas. In spring, the concentration is even more dramatic; 75 percent of all the birds were at just two sites! And more than 90 percent of the White-rumped, Baird's, and Stilt Sandpipers, Long-billed Dowitchers and Wilson's Phalaropes counted in April and May were almost always at one site: Cheyenne Bottoms, Kansas.

Red-necked Phalarope juvenile

Likewise, 80 percent of the Ruddy Turnstones and Red Knots counted were noted along the Delaware Bay shoreline, where they were joined by 70 percent of the Semipalmated Sandpipers and 60 percent of the Sanderlings.

Seeing tens, even hundreds of thousands of shorebirds at a single site would seem to indicate that the species present are in no danger at all. But these amazing concentrations leave entire populations vulnerable to disaster.

Delaware Bay is the largest oil transfer port-of-entry on the East Coast. An oil spill there—like the one in the opening scenario—would be devastating to hundreds of thousands of shorebirds dependent on horseshoe crab eggs. The "fuel" (fat) that the birds take on there powers not only their flight to the Far North, but sustains them for a week or more once they reach their breeding locales.

Dwindling water supplies (caused by diversion of water for irrigation) threaten many important inland stopover sites like Cheyenne Bottoms, Mono Lake, and the Lahontan Valley. At many such sites, recent conservation victories assured wetlands of minimum water levels, but recent long-term droughts have left both rivers and wetlands bone dry.

THE GOOD NEWS

The work of hundreds of ISS cooperators at more than 500 sites in both North and South America is tremendously important to shorebird conservation efforts in the New World. Without the data gathered by both professional and amateur researchers, even the most influential conservation organizations would be powerless.

ISS supplies data to a number of refuges so that the needs of shorebirds may be met as plans for future management are developed. It works with other governmental and conservation agencies on specific shorebird conservation issues such as off-road vehicle use in staging areas, control of water levels at manmade impoundments, dwindling water supplies at inland locations, and the threatened development of critical sites.

The Western Hemisphere Shorebird Reserve Network (WHSRN) is a voluntary collaboration of private and government organizations committed to protecting shorebirds and their wetlands habitats. It was formed in 1985 to address alarming declines in shorebird numbers and to support local wetlands conservation efforts by focusing international attention on local issues and problems. Though actually a Wetlands for the Americas (WA) program, WHSRN is currently funded by Manomet Observatory, Wildlife Habitat Canada, the U.S. Fish and

Marbled Godwit in breeding plumage

Wildlife Service, and several foundations.

Today, nine national agencies as well as 32 state or provincial wildlife agencies have made commitments to support the Western Hemisphere Shorebird Reserve Network. In a single decade, 31 critical stopover sites have been nominated for inclusion in the network, ensuring the protection of 25 million acres of wetlands and 30 million shorebirds.

Manomet Observatory and Wetlands for the Americas continues working to expand ISS and WHSRN programs in South America, where most of our migratory shorebirds winter. Various workshops and projects dealing with shorebird conservation and research have been conducted in Argentina, Brazil, Chile, Costa Rica, Ecuador, Mexico, Peru, and Suriname. As a result, many important staging areas have been identified and government awareness in all of South America has increased. Important staging areas in Argentina, Brazil, Peru, and Suriname have already been designated as WHSRN sites.

How You Can Help

Birders across North America can help by continuing to support those conservation agencies—like The Nature Conservancy and local Audubon Society chapters, among others—that work to protect wetlands and coastal areas from disturbance, destruction, development, and pollution.

By keeping accurate field notes for one or more local sites and forwarding your counts to the ISS, you can contribute substantially to our understanding of shorebird populations and movements. ISS Director Brian Harrington explains that no site is too small, and even large sites that harbor few birds need to be surveyed: "In order to better understand where they are, we have to know where they aren't."

Lastly, anybody who peers through a scope can help by searching for color-banded shorebirds. Try to record the complete band combination, and be sure to note the color of the leg flag, which is a color band with a short tab, or extension. The leg flag denotes the country in which the bird was banded. I have seen blue-flagged birds (Brazil) in New Jersey, orange- (Argentina) and white- (Canada)

Sanderling molting to breeeding plumage

flagged birds in New York, and green-flagged birds (banded in the USA) on three coasts!

To record band data start with the left leg above the tarsus, then below. Then do the same with the right leg. Record steel or aluminum Fish & Wildlife bands as "M" (for metal), and leg flags as FL with the flag color as a lower-case abbreviation. For example: RY, M: , FL (wh) indicates a bird with both red and yellow color bands on the left leg above the tarsus, a metal band below, no bands on the right leg above the tarsus, and a white flag below.

Once you get good at it you can save lots of time and space by making a diagram like this:

```
R |
Y |_____
__|_____
M | FL (wh)
```

Sightings of color-banded shorebirds should be reported to Dr. Cheri Gratto-Trevor, Pan American Shorebird Program, Canadian Wildlife Service, 115 Perimeter Road, Saskatoon, Saskatchewan, S7N 0X4 Canada. Along with the band data, include the date, time, and location of the sighting, and if possible, the types and approximate numbers of other shorebirds present. Such reports are of great help to those conducting research projects designed to unravel the mysteries of shorebird migration.

Watching, studying, identifying, counting, photographing, and writing about shorebirds can be fun, educational, challenging, satisfying and thrilling.

One can only wonder about their wanderings: how does a young Pectoral Sandpiper raised in central-northern Russia find its way to Argentina?

One can only wonder about their survival: how does a baby American Golden-Plover elude a hungry arctic fox? How does a driveway-raised Killdeer chick evade the wheels of the family car?

And one can only wonder: what does a returning Willet think when it finds that the marsh it bred in last year is now a shopping mall?

Humans play an important role in the survival of shorebirds. Only we can ensure that they will be flying to the ends of the earth in centuries to come.

For More Information

Bird Banding Laboratory
12100 Beech Forest Road
Laurel, MD 20708
www.pwrc.usgs.gov/bbl

Canadian Wildlife Service
351 St. Joseph Boulevard
Hull, Quebec K1A 0H3
Canada
www.cws-scf.ec.gc.ca

Cape May Bird Observatory
P.O. Box 3
Cape May Point, NJ 08212
www.njaudubon.org/Centers/CMBO

International Shorebird Survery
c/o Manomet Observatory
P.O. Box 1770
Manomet, MA 02345

Manomet Observatory
P.O. Box 1770
Manomet, MA 02345
www.manomet.org

Wader Study Group
The National Centre for Ornithology
The Nannery, Thetford
Norfolk JP24 2PU
United Kingdom
www.wadestudygroup.org

Western Hemisphere Shorebird
   Reserve Network
c/o Manomet Observatory
P.O. Box 1770
Manomet, MA 02345
www.manomet.org/WHSRN

Wetlands for the Americas
Monroe 2142
1428 Buenos Aires
Argentina
www.wetlands.org

Plover-prints

Suggested Reading

Bent, Arthur Cleveland. 1927. *Life Histories of North American Shorebirds (Part 1)*. U.S. National Museum.

———. 1927. *Life Histories of North American Shorebirds (Part 2)*. U.S. National Museum.

Bull, John and John Farrand, Jr. 1994. *National Audubon Society Field Guide to North American Birds: Eastern Region*. New York: Alfred A. Knopf.

———. 1994. *National Audubon Society Field Guide to North American Birds: Western Region*. New York: Alfred A. Knopf.

Cramp, S. and K. E. L. Simmons. 1983. *The Birds of the Western Palearctic, Vol. 3: Waders to Gulls*. Oxford: Oxford University Press.

Chandler, Richard J. 1989. *North Atlantic Shorebirds*. New York: Facts on File.

Farrand, John Jr. 1977. *The Audubon Society Master Guide to Birding, Volume 1: Loons to Sandpipers*. New York: Alfred A. Knopf.

Hayman, Peter, John Marchant and Tony Prater. 1986. *Shorebirds: An Identification Guide to the Waders of the World*. Boston: Houghton Mifflin.

Harrington, Brian A. with Charles Flowers. 1996. *The Flight of the Red Knot*. New York: W. W. Norton.

Johnsgard, Paul A. 1981. *The Plovers, Sandpipers, and Snipes of the World*. Lincoln: University of Nebraska Press.

Kaufman, Ken. 1990. *A Field Guide to Advanced Birding*. Boston: Houghton Mifflin Co.

Matthiessen, Peter. 1973. *The Wind Birds*. New York: Viking Press.

National Geographic Society. 1987. *Field Guide to the Birds of North America*. Washington, D.C.

Paulson, Dennis. 1993. *Shorebirds of the Pacific Northwest*. University of British Colombia: UBC Press.

Peterson, Roger Tory. 1980. *A Field Guide to Eastern Birds*. Boston: Houghton Mifflin Co.

———. 1990. *A Field Guide to Western Birds*. Boston: Houghton Mifflin Co.

Poole, Alan and Frank B. Gill (eds.) *The Birds of North America*. Philadelphia: The Academy of Natural Sciences.

Richards, Alan. 1988. *Shorebirds: A Complete Guide to Their Behavior and Migration*. New York: Gallery Books.

Robbins, Chandler S., Bertel Bruun and Herbert S. Zim. 1983. *A Guide to Field Identification: Birds of North America*. New York: Golden Press.

Stokes, Donald and Lillian. 1996. S*tokes' Field Guide to the Birds: Eastern Region*. New York: Little, Brown and Company.

———. 1996. S*tokes' Field Guide to the Birds: Western Region*. New York: Little, Brown and Company.

Terres, John K. 1980. *The Audubon Society Encyclopedia of North American Birds*. New York: Alfred A. Knopf.

PHOTO INDEX

with months indicated

Avocet, American — title page, 94, 144: June

Curlew, Long-billed — 106-7: Feb

Dowitcher, Long-billed — 20-21: Apr; 46: Oct
Dowitcher, Short-billed — 23: May; 25: Nov; 135: Sept
Dunlin — 129: May

Godwit, Hudsonian — 49: June; 108: Oct
Godwit, Marbled — 9: June; 71: Jan; 109: Dec; 150: June; back cover: Aug
Golden-Plover, Pacific — TOC: Sept
Golden-Plover, American — 34: Sept; 63, 80: June; 65: July

Killdeer — 88: Mar
Knot, Red — 26: Sept; 28: Nov; 29, 69, 157: May; 73: Feb

Oystercatcher, American — 22, 55: Mar; 90-91: Apr; 154-55: May
Oystercatcher, Black — 74: Dec

Phalarope, Red — 52: June
Phalarope, Red-necked — 140: June; 149: Sept
Phalarope, Wilson's — 15, 62, 139: June
Plover, Black-bellied — dedication page: Dec; 40: June; 44-45: July; 78: Sept
Plover, Mountain — 89: Nov
Plover, Piping — 67: May; 86-87: Apr
Plover, Semipalmated — 85: June
Plover, Snowy — 82-83: Feb
Plover, Wilson's — 84: Mar

Ruff — 133: June

Sanderling — 43: May; 33: Oct; 41, 42: Sept; 152: Apr
Sandpiper, Baird's — 123: Sept
Sandpiper, Buff-breasted — 53, 54: June
Sandpiper, Curlew — 131: July
Sandpiper, Least — 30, 37, 121: Aug
Sandpiper, Pectoral — 59: June; 124-25: Sept
Sandpiper, Purple — 127: Feb
Sandpiper, Rock — 128: July
Sandpiper, Semipalmated — 38: Sept; 117: July
Sandpiper, Stilt — 11: Aug; 12: June
Sandpiper, Solitary — 101: May
Sandpiper, Spotted — 60: June
Sandpiper, Upland — 105: Apr
Sandpipers, Western — 76-77: May; 119: July
Sandpiper, White-rumped — 122: Sept
Snipe, Common — 137: Sept
Stilt, Black-necked — 66: Apr; 93: June.
Stint, Red-necked — 13: May
Surfbird — 114: Jan

Tattler, Wandering — 103: Dec
Turnstone, Black — 112: Jan
Turnstone, Ruddy — 111, 157: May

Whimbrel — 35: Jan
Willet — cover, 57: June
Woodcock, American — 138: May

Yellowlegs, Greater — 96-97: Sept
Yellowlegs, Lesser — 50: June; 98-99: July